Equality with a Vengeance

The Northeastern Series on Gender, Crime, and Law
Editor: Claire Renzetti

For a complete list of books available in this series, please visit www.upne.com

Men's Rights
Groups,
Battered Women,
and
Antifeminist
Backlash

Equality
with a Vengeance

Molly Dragiewicz

Northeastern University Press | BOSTON

Northeastern University Press
Published by University Press of New England
www.upne.com
© 2011 Northeastern University
All rights reserved
Manufactured in the United States of America
Designed by Katherine B. Kimball
Typeset in Minion by Integrated Publishing Solutions

University Press of New England is a member of the
Green Press Initiative. The paper used in this book
meets their minimum requirement for recycled paper.

For permission to reproduce any of the material in this
book, contact Permissions, University Press of New
England, One Court Street, Suite 250, Lebanon NH
03766; or visit www.upne.com

Library of Congress Cataloging-in-Publication Data
Dragiewicz, Molly.
Equality with a vengeance / Molly Dragiewicz.
    p. cm. — (The Northeastern series on gender,
crime, and law)
Includes bibliographical references and index.
ISBN 978-1-55553-738-8 (cloth : alk. paper) —
ISBN 978-1-55553-739-5 (pbk. : alk. paper) —
ISBN 978-1-55553-756-2 (e-book : alk. paper)
1. Abused women—United States. 2. Family
violence—United States. 3. Family violence—Law
and legislation—United States. 4. Feminism—
United States. I. Title.
HV6626.2.D74 2011
344.7303'28292—dc22   2010047810

5 4 3 2 1

This book is dedicated to the survivors
who have taught me everything I really know about
woman abuse. Your strength, wisdom, and resilience are
a constant source of inspiration for me.

Contents

Acknowledgments

I can't begin to articulate the appreciation I feel for the many people who have contributed in some way to the completion of this book. One of the many rewarding aspects of working on violence and gender is having the privilege to spend time with the amazing group of people who do this work. I am truly fortunate to have such brilliant friends, mentors, and colleagues. This book would not have been possible without help from Loretta Frederick, who sent me a huge box of photocopies from the *Booth v. Hvass* case almost ten years ago.

I would like to thank Susan Boyd, Susan Caringella, Glynis Carr, Sarah Deer, Walter DeKeseredy, Myra Dinnerstein, Marc Dubin, Kim Eby, Marci Fukuroda, Shannon Garrett, Leigh Goodmark, Annika Gifford, Paula Gilbert, Barry Goldstein, Lisa Gring-Pemble, Barbara Hart, Mo Hannah, Lorna Irvine, Roger Lancaster, Anne Menard, Sue Osthoff, Ellen Pence, Mary Koss, Nancy Lemon, Yvette Lindgren, Joan Meier, Patti Jo Newell, Marty Schwartz, Dan Saunders, Natalie Sokoloff, Zina Santos, Tara Shabazz, Rita Smith, Sue Tompkins, Rob Valente, Rebecca Walter, Joan Zorza, and everyone from the American Society of Criminology Division on Women and Crime, CAVNET and FIVERS. I would also like to thank Phyllis Deutsch, editor-in-chief at University Press of New England and Claire Renzetti, series editor for the Northeastern Series on Gender, Crime, and Law, for their patience, advice, and encouragement. A huge thank you is due to Kathryn Grover for her careful copyediting and suggestions, which have contributed greatly to the final manuscript. Thanks to Lori Miller, Barbara Briggs, Katy Grabill, Christine Hauck, Sherri Strickland, Deborah Forward, and David Corey at the University Press of New England for assistance with production and marketing. Thank you also to the Domestic Abuse Intervention Project for granting permission to reprint the power and control wheel. I look forward to continuing work in this area with all of you. Finally, I would like to thank Matt Brenner, Judy Dragiewicz,

Larry Dragiewicz, Marc Dragiewicz, Robert Carlson, and Shirley Carlson for all of their love and support.

This book contains material adapted from earlier publications including Molly Dragiewicz 2008, "Patriarchy Reasserted: Fathers' Rights and Anti-VAWA Activism," *Feminist Criminology* 3, 2: 121–44, and Molly Dragiewicz 2009, "Why Sex and Gender Matter in Domestic Violence Research and Advocacy," in *Violence Against Women in Families and Relationships*, vol. 3, *Criminal Justice and the Law*, eds. Evan Stark and Eve S. Buzawa, pp. 201–16 (Santa Barbara, CA: Praeger).

Equality with a Vengeance

Introduction

On October 17, 2000, eighteen men sued the Commissioner of Corrections, Commissioner of Human Services, Commissioner of Public Safety, and Commissioner of Children, Families and Learning for the state of Minnesota to eliminate the mechanism for dispersal of state and federal funding for battered women's shelters and other services for domestic abuse victims and their children in Minnesota.[1] *Booth v. Hvass* argued,

> The said battered women's shelters . . . publish fanatical, irrational, hysterical, sexist literature which maliciously and falsely defames and seeks to generate social and political hatred against men in general, portraying them as the basic cause of all domestic violence and associated acts of cruelty in American society. (Amended complaint 2000, 4)

The lawsuit identified the plaintiffs as affiliates of three antifeminist groups, the R-KIDS Legal Action Committee, the Men's Defense Association, and the National Coalition of Free Men, Twin Cities Chapter.[2] The plaintiffs demanded that the set of Minnesota statutes they referred to as the "Minnesota Battered Women's Act" be declared unconstitutional and "null and void as if never passed" (Amended complaint 2000, 8).[3] Accordingly, the *Booth* plaintiffs demanded an injunction forbidding the promotion of any objectives of the state's domestic abuse statutes, including provision of emergency shelter, prevention education, legal assistance, and other services. The legal basis of the lawsuit was an equal protection claim premised on the allegation that women and men are "similarly situated" with regard to domestic violence.[4] The plaintiffs claimed that the cited Minnesota statutes on domestic violence and abuse result in the "oppression of husbands, fathers, and men in general" (Amended complaint 2000, 8; Minnesota statutes 2000, citing sections 611A.31–611A.36).

The first equal protection lawsuit that attacked funding for domestic violence shelters and other services in the United States, *Booth v. Hvass*

1

sought to institutionalize a gender-blind understanding of what it termed "domestic violence" by eliminating the mechanism for dispersal of state and federal funding for organizations working on the issue, including emergency shelters and antiviolence advocacy groups such as the Domestic Abuse Intervention Project. The lawsuit also criticized the availability of legal remedies for violence perpetrated by intimates. The *Booth* plaintiffs specifically objected to the availability and enforcement of orders for protection and complained that advocates assisted women in applying for such orders (Amended complaint 2000, 3). Overall, the plaintiffs argued that Minnesota's funding of domestic violence programs and services "aids in the publication of sexist defamation, creating hatred against a class of persons of which they are members and a prejudicial atmosphere against such class of persons in state courts of justice in Minnesota" (Plaintiffs' answer to interrogatories 2001, 8). As these assertions illustrate, the plaintiffs regarded changes in the discourse on violence and gender as an important goal.

Efforts to excise gender from discourses on woman abuse in order to claim that domestic violence is gender-neutral crystallized in *Booth v. Hvass*. Because the context, history, and power relations involved in violence against women and men are of primary significance in the etiology of and responses to violence, the trend to ignore gender has harmful implications (Bograd 1990b; DeKeseredy 2000; Dobash et al. 1992; Gilligan 1997 and 2001; Johnson and Ferraro 2000). The *Booth* plaintiffs' legal argument that women and men are similarly situated with regard to domestic violence confuses sex, a biological category, and gender, a social and cultural construct; it alternates between assertions that violence is sex-symmetrical and claims that patriarchal gender norms are irrelevant to violence.

Backlash

Appeals to remove gender from conversations about woman abuse are part of a broader backlash against feminism (DeKeseredy and Dragiewicz 2007). Susan Faludi coined the term "backlash" to describe the "cultural counterreaction" against feminism in which each feminist effort to advance women's rights has been met with a counterattack seeking to undermine and reverse feminist gains (1991, 48). Popular culture is one important location of antifeminist backlash. Faludi noted that popular discourses proclaim that feminism is no longer needed because the United

States has already achieved the goal of women's equality. At the same time, myriad social problems indicating that women's efforts to attain equality have not yet been successful are attributed to feminism rather than to persistent inequalities.

Faludi observed that "the backlash remarkets old myths about women as new facts and ignores all appeals to reason" (xxii). This passage aptly describes recent efforts by antifeminist groups to portray woman abuse as a degendered phenomenon, twin to "husband battering." In the face of evidence from sources as disparate as hospital emergency rooms, the courts, domestic violence shelters, homicide records, scholars, antiviolence advocates, and police departments, all pointing to the gendered dynamics of violence, some individuals and organizations insist that violence against intimates is gender-neutral. Although Faludi's account focuses on mass-mediated representations of feminism, efforts to reverse the gains of feminism are also visible in scholarship, law, and politics.

Michel Foucault argued that discourses are used to create and maintain social control, that "men govern (themselves and others) by the production of truth" (Foucault 1987, 108). The truths that govern, however, do not represent all interests equally well. The truths produced by some discourses on violence harm women by blaming them for it, justifying its occurrence, and excusing the community's failure to act against it. Recent legal attacks against shelters serving battered women have relied upon such discourses as part of a political effort to roll back the successes of the battered women's movement.[5] Although antifeminist groups claim that violence against women has nothing to do with patriarchy, their activism focuses on the changes to law they see as detrimental to patriarchal families, including changes in domestic violence law and policy (Dragiewicz 2008; Rosen, Dragiewicz, and Gibbs 2009). Campaigns to eliminate discussion of the role of persistent, gendered, structural inequalities in violence seek to silence the questions about patriarchy explicitly raised by the battered women's movement and implicit in public efforts to assist battered women.

The United States District Court, District of Minnesota, Third Division dismissed *Booth v. Hvass* in 2001. The United States Court of Appeals for the Eighth Circuit upheld the dismissal in 2002, and in 2003 the Supreme Court of the United States declined to hear the case. Still, *Booth v. Hvass* offers a case study of contemporary efforts to impose gender-blind understandings of domestic violence in reaction to the availability of resources helpful to battered women. Such efforts advance claims about domestic violence as gender-neutral in two senses—genderless (neuter) and generic (nonspecific). In contrast to these propositions, I review the *Booth* plaintiffs' claims in the context of the empirical research indicating that violence is profoundly and pervasively gendered.

The primary objective of this book is to examine the arguments the *Booth* plaintiffs and other antifeminist men's groups make in efforts to undermine the laws and resources abused women use and to explore the relationship of such efforts to a more generalized backlash against feminism in the United States. Antifeminist groups have brought and supported multiple lawsuits attacking the existence of domestic violence shelters, challenging the enforcement of domestic violence laws, and seeking to eliminate the funding sources that support them (Dragiewicz and Lindgren 2009). However, to date no book has examined these lawsuits or addressed their relationship to discourses on and responses to woman abuse more generally. Despite the legal failure of *Booth v. Hvass*, the lawsuit foreshadowed later cases. Furthermore, as Martha Fineman argued,

> When social norms are in a state of flux (as they certainly are in regard to matters of sexual intimacy and gender relations) the law tends to become identified as a significant site of contest. Competing societal factions seek to codify their worldview, thereby giving legitimacy to the stories they tell about what are appropriate ideals and values. Policy formation and law reform in this regard are inevitably political or, at least, tend to develop in a politicized environment. This is significant because it means that the lawmaking (or law-interpreting) process often becomes a highly charged, symbolic endeavor signaling who wins and who loses in an ongoing battle over larger societal definitions and directions. (1994, xii–xiii)

The *Booth* case is one such site, as are other legal challenges to the laws and services abused women rely upon. Even more important than the outcome in any particular case is what such lawsuits as *Booth v. Hvass* can reveal about implicit, deeply ingrained assumptions about the appropriate boundaries of efforts to address violence against women. Where do our values in favor of nonviolence intersect with values preserving patriarchy? How do these competing values play out in practice? How are mainstream conceptualizations of social problems codified in the law?

This book makes three key contributions to the literature. First, it explains how misuse of the concept of equal protection has the potential to impact policies affecting battered women negatively by imposing gender-blind conceptions of a gendered social problem. Second, it makes connections between *Booth v. Hvass*, other antifeminist discourses on woman abuse, and batterer narratives in order to illustrate the extent to which the failure to account for patriarchal gender norms and structures is pervasive and problematic. Third, it explains the difference between sex, gender, and patriarchy and reviews the research evidence that shows how each is relevant to understanding woman abuse.

My Position as a Scholar

Louise Armstrong and Leonard Tennenhouse argued that "to regard certain practices as violent is never to see them just as they are. It is always to take up a position for or against them" (1989, 9). Unlike those who characterize "advocacy research" as political rather than scholarly, I recognize that all knowledge is political and either affirms or challenges existing hierarchies of power. Abdicating responsibility for the political implications of one's research does not eliminate those implications. To claim that all knowledge is political does not mean that all knowledge is relative or that all knowledges are equally valid. When investigating a problem as complex as violence, it is necessary to examine evidence from across the vast, interdisciplinary body of research. My research on woman abuse and other forms of violence is driven by the pragmatic need for policy and practice in the interest of intervention and, ultimately, prevention. My interests in research on violence and abuse are driven by the needs of survivors of violence and those who would assist them. As such, I am a scholar and antiviolence advocate.

Chapter Outline

In chapter 1, I establish the political context for *Booth v. Hvass*. Because terminology is so central to debates about woman abuse and violence policy, I first review the history of terminological debates and define the terms used in this book. Then, I introduce the scholarly and political contexts for the emergence of federal policy on violence against women in the United States. Next, I situate antifeminist men's groups within their contemporary social and political context.

In chapter 2, I examine *Booth v. Hvass*. This chapter focuses on the merits, or substantive issues, of the case to elucidate the plaintiffs' claims, enumerate the demands made to address these claims, and evaluate the documentation provided as evidence to support the plaintiffs' position.

The claims made in the *Booth* case are relevant to a variety of discourses circulating beyond the lawsuit. Although the rhetoric in the complaint is sometimes extreme and incoherent, it draws from mainstream anti-feminist understandings of violence and abuse. Despite the *Booth* plaintiffs' assertions that research proves women and men are similarly situated with regard to violence and abuse, I show how the very sources they cited not only fail to support but actually undermine this argument. Finally, this chapter reviews the respondents' documentation in support of the existing Minnesota laws and services.

In chapter 3, I connect the claims and arguments made in *Booth v. Hvass* with other discourses on woman abuse. Drawing on the extant research on media and scholarly discourses on violence against women, I outline common feminist and antifeminist frames found in discourses about woman abuse. This chapter illustrates how, despite their efforts to position themselves as promoting an up-to-date, scientific view of domestic violence, the *Booth* plaintiffs simply recycle antifeminist frames commonly found in popular and scholarly media.

In chapter 4, in order to provide additional context for *Booth v. Hvass*, I show how men's accounts of perpetrating violence against women relate to other discourses. I draw upon the published research on batterer narratives to describe well-documented patterns in their accounts of violence against women. These patterns reveal striking similarities between batterers' accounts and the claims antifeminist activists make about symmetry in domestic violence. The batterer narratives also demonstrate the importance of patriarchal gender norms to batterers, which contradicts *Booth*'s claim that men's violence against women is not a gender issue.

In chapter 5, I examine the research basis of assertions about the sex symmetry of domestic violence made in *Booth v. Hvass* and repeated in other contexts. This chapter centers on the types of research cited in the case to examine what it can and cannot tell us about woman abuse and other forms of violence. Chapter 5 also reviews current empirical research refuting sex-symmetry claims.

In chapter 6, I explain the difference between sex and gender and explain why it matters for understanding woman abuse and other forms of violence. I discuss what feminists mean when they talk about patriarchy as a contributing factor to violence and articulate an ecological model for patriarchy as it contributes to violence against women. In this section, I show how the documents submitted by the *Booth* plaintiffs and the antifeminist discourses from which they borrow inadvertently yet strongly support the importance of gender.

Finally, in chapter 7, I argue that, regardless of the intent of such rhetoric, discourses proclaiming sex symmetry in violence against intimates serve to reproduce the conditions that enable violence by silencing those most adversely affected, obscuring structural contributing factors, and echoing abusers. Referring again to the research on media, scholarly, and batterer narratives, I analyze the points of overlap between *Booth v. Hvass* and other antifeminist approaches to woman abuse. I also review the limitations of this inquiry and make recommendations for future research. I conclude by presenting recommendations for responsible policy and practice that take the research on woman abuse, violence, and gender into account.

1 | Key Contexts

Terminology

The World Health Organization's *World Report on Violence and Health* (2002) concisely summarized the difficulties of defining violence:

> Violence is an extremely diffuse and complex phenomenon. Defining it is not an exact science but a matter of judgement. Notions of what is acceptable and unacceptable in terms of behaviour, and what constitutes harm, are culturally influenced and constantly under review as values and social norms evolve. (4)

These difficulties apply to definitions of woman abuse. The emergence of multiple forms of violence against women into public consciousness is evidence of a successful feminist political campaign. However, mainstream awareness of violence against intimate partners has come at a price, including, arguably, the widespread use of the term, "domestic violence." Kathleen Ferraro wrote,

> [Domestic violence] discourse is a feminist victory, on one side, as it has urged social recognition of women's oppression and developed material resources and institutions specifically addressed to the problem. It is simultaneously a feminist nightmare, as it has absorbed grassroots struggles into the machinery of social engineering and mass mediation, reinscribing patterns of race, class, and gender domination. (1996, 77)

Ferraro argued that the term domestic violence "glosses the intricate, layered connections of power relationships built on race, class, and gender hierarchies, each tied in unique fashion to requirements of female dependency" (1996, 77). While a substantial portion of the gloss described here is due to white, heterosexual, and middle-class feminist failures to integrate analyses of race, class, and sexuality alongside critiques of gender

(Davis 2000), another part of the conflict comes from the intersection of feminist emancipatory ideals with mainstream conservative impulses (Ferraro 1996). Because representations of abused women as innocent victims deserving of protection do not challenge stereotypes about women as weak and dependent on men, it is possible to take a position against domestic violence while supporting the institutions and conditions that engender it (Kozol 1995, Meyers 1997). Debates over terminology illustrate the struggle over contradictory approaches to the problem of violence against women.

Debates about terminology are also instructive because they reveal issues that are central to discussions of violence and gender. Feminists have proposed a variety of terms for woman abuse, have carefully considered the positive and negative ramifications of each term, and have agonized over issues such as the use of sex-specific or sex-neutral words, the inclusion of marriage-related terms, and the connotations of each option (Gordon 1988; Kurz 1993; Meyers 1997; Pleck et al. 1977–78; Websdale 1998). R. Emerson Dobash and Russell Dobash summarized these debates in their book *Women, Violence and Social Change*:

> The movements continue to debate and refine the terms used to define the problem, the organisations and the individuals involved. Is the problem wife abuse or woman abuse? Wife abuse implies that the social institution of marriage as well as gender is central, but has the drawback that it may also imply that violence is only directed at women living in the legal, rather than the social state of marriage. Woman abuse focuses on gender and avoids the problem of assuming legal marriage but, in so doing, loses emphasis upon the analytical insight that the social institution of marriage as traditionally constructed forms much of the foundation of the problem.... Beating and battering may be more descriptive, but are they too literal and emotive? As descriptive terms, domestic, spousal and family violence obscure the gendered nature of the problem and ignore the relationship involved. (1992, 38–39)

All of these terms have benefits and drawbacks, and each categorization scheme reflects unique interests and values. No term is perfect. What is at stake in choosing and defining terminology is the prescribed outcome, or "truth effects," of the discourse (Foucault 1972). Celeste Condit argued that the meanings media audiences are likely to attribute to social issues are circumscribed by the language and information already in circulation in their social environment (1989). Thus, establishing and legitimating terminology are political acts that institute the terms of a discourse and determine to an extent its possibilities and effects (Bograd 1990a; Kurz 1993). Chris Weedon similarly argued that the discourses available at any given time help to determine how people interpret the world around them, "for example, the way in which a woman experiences and responds to domestic violence will depend on the ways of understanding to which she has access" (1987, 76). In other words, the production of discourse on woman abuse is political because it is part of the negotiation that accompanies the deployment of knowledge (Yl10 1990).

Like many scholars, I argue that it is important to acknowledge the different dynamics of multiple forms of violence while also recognizing common contributing factors. Scholars and advocates need to be clear about the type of violence they are writing about because failing to do so can result in inappropriate generalizations from one type of violence to another or other inaccurate conclusions (Johnson and Ferraro 2000). In this book, I focus on the problem of woman abuse. Woman abuse refers to the pattern of abuse and coercive control (Stark 2007) men exercise over female intimate partners in which physical violence, threats of violence, sexual assault, verbal abuse, and psychological abuse tend to coincide. I use the term woman abuse to denote the wide range of abusive behaviors that constitute the context of physical violence. Woman abuse frequently includes isolation of the victim from family and friends, restricted mobility, threats of violence, and withholding resources that might enable a victim to leave. I include domestic homicides in the category of woman abuse because, although relatively rare, they comprise a third of all homicides of women (Fox and Zawitz 2010).

Woman abuse is commonly connoted by the term "domestic violence." However, the term domestic violence may not be completely clear because it is also sometimes used to refer to other forms of violence in the family, including child abuse and elder abuse. Domestic violence also obscures sex and gender differences and can contribute to a misleading impression that the dynamics of violence and abuse are the same for women and men. This book is focused on woman abuse because it is the kind of abuse that battered women's shelters were created to address, and these are the resources that *Booth v. Hvass* attacked.

Research

Research on violence against women has proliferated since the inception of the battered women's movement in the United States in the 1970s. Prior to the 1970s, research on violence against women was much less common than it is today (Foundational publications included Brownmiller 1975; Gordon 1988; Koss, Gidycz, and Wisniewski 1987; Martin 1981; Pagelow 1981; Russell 1982; Schechter 1982). Studies have evolved from early attempts to describe and quantify the problem to a wide-ranging field of inquiry that examines every possible facet of the correlated factors of, causes of, and responses to violence against women. The growth of the research literature is illustrated by the peer-reviewed journal dedicated to the issue, *Violence Against Women*. Following its creation in 1995, the journal rapidly expanded. The journal was published four times a year in 1995, six times a year by 1997, and monthly by 2000. In 1996 *Essential Science Indicators*, Thompson Reuters' citation tracking program, named it a "rising star" because it was so frequently cited. *Violence Against Women* is now ranked in the top 50 percent of social science journals for citation (In-Cites 2006), which indicates the rapidly increasing scientific importance of research in this area.

Feminist perspectives on gender as a salient factor in understanding violence have also gained visibility and influence over time. *Booth v. Hvass* is after all an explicit reaction against what the plaintiffs perceived as the popular conception that "domestic violence" means men beating women. A handful of scholars claim that "in Canada and the United States, women use violence in intimate relationships to the same extent as men, for the same reasons, and with largely the same results" (Dutton 2006, ix), but these perspectives are increasingly marginal in the interdisciplinary field of violence research. The majority of scholars who object to the feminist emphasis on gender do not endorse the idea that the violence women and men experience in relationships has similar dynamics or outcomes. Instead, the debates appear to be disputes about feminism and the importance accorded to patriarchy (Archer 2000a; DeKeseredy 1996; DeKeseredy and Dragiewicz 2007; Dutton 2006; Gelles 1999; Straus 1993).

In the years since feminists struggled to secure the recognition of woman abuse as a social problem in need of a community response and researchers began to study the problem, feminist insights have been incorporated into almost every possible context. For example, the American Medical Association has published guidelines advocating that public health research distinguish between sex and gender and clearly reflect these differences in its language. This directive reflects the feminist articulation of the distinction between biological sex and gender as "culturally and socially shaped variations between men and women" (American Medical Association 2000). Recognition of the gendered nature of violence is increasingly stressed by such international organizations as the World Health Organization, which has highlighted the importance of gender inequality in contributing to the observed sex differences in violence and in other public health problems (World Health Organization 2002).

These developments indicate that feminism's influence on discussions about certain forms of violence is pervasive. Arguably, the infiltration of emancipatory concepts into mainstream discourses has been a process of assimilation rather than revolution. Dominant discourses often incorporate a collection of contradictory messages about women, men, and violence (Meyers 1997). Over the past fifty years, hundreds of books and articles on violence and abuse have offered a myriad of approaches and perspectives. This outpouring of research has added greatly to the visibility of violence against women in the public sphere, but it has not completely supplanted the rhetoric that preceded it.

Advocates have used the burgeoning research literature on the prevalence and seriousness of violence effectively to argue for public funding of a range of services for battered women including emergency shelters, hotlines, websites, and legal support systems to address the problem (Valente et al. 2001). Among the most visible recent examples of these changes are federal policy initiatives such as the 1994 Violence Against Women Act (VAWA).

Policy

Although VAWA is the best-known federal law addressing domestic violence, it was not the first effort to institutionalize a federal response to the problem in the United States. National domestic violence bills were introduced and defeated in 1977 and 1978. President Jimmy Carter established an Office of Domestic Violence in 1979, which President Ronald Reagan closed after he was elected (Brooks 1997, 68). Intermittent efforts to introduce federal legislation on domestic violence continued until then-Senator Joseph Biden introduced VAWA in 1990 (Brooks 1997, 69).

The passage of VAWA effectively institutionalized support for emergency services and law enforcement for battered women at the federal level (Dragiewicz 2008; Valente et al. 2001). Because VAWA was passed as part of an omnibus crime bill—it is Title IV of the Violent Crime Control and Law Enforcement Act of 1994 (Public Law 103–322)—its funding has prioritized policing and other justice-system responses to violence. Originally Congress appropriated $800,000,000 over six years for training grants for law enforcement, $325,000,000 over six years for battered women's shelters, and an additional $12,000,000 over six years for programs encouraging arrest (Brooks 1997, 76–77). Although prevention and other initiatives were also included in VAWA, they were funded at much lower levels. These funding priorities make the federal focus on emergency services and law enforcement quite clear.

Although individual members of Congress lobby for amendments at each renewal, VAWA has consistently received overwhelming endorsement. It passed out of the Senate by unanimous consent as part of the Violence Against Women and Department of Justice Reauthorization Act of 2005 (Public Law 109–162) and won nearly unanimous congressional support as Division B of the Victims of Trafficking and Violence Protection Act of 2000 (Public Law 106–386) (Laney 2005). Government recognition of pervasive public support for emergency services and legal protection for battered women represents a profound and rapid change in attitudes toward violence against women in the United States (Valente et al. 2001). At the very least, what was previously seen as a private family issue has come to be seen as a crime. The change from private dispute to public social problem has posed a serious ideological challenge for antifeminist activists in the United States (Dragiewicz 2008).

Antifeminist "Men's Rights" and "Fathers' Rights" Groups

In the United States, Canada, Australia, and the United Kingdom, "men's rights" or "fathers' rights" groups have been among the most vocal critics of laws and policies designed to protect battered women (Chunn et al. 2007; Collier and Sheldon 2006; Dragiewicz 2008; Flood 2010; Girard 2009; Mann 2008). Fathers' rights groups could be considered a branch of the men's rights movement, and the activities and interests of the groups overlap considerably (Flood 2010; Williams and Williams 1995).

Although resistance to feminism has a long history, the adoption of the men's and fathers' rights labels is a relatively recent phenomenon. The most recent wave of groups advocating for "men's rights" appeared in the late 1960s in response both to divorce reform and the rising feminist movement (Chesler 1994; Crowley 2009; Dragiewicz 2008; Menzies 2007). Phyllis Chesler (1994) noted that men's and fathers' rights groups grew out of the fissures between feminist efforts to involve men in parenting and antifeminist efforts to reinforce the patriarchal nuclear family; such groups repackaged "long–standing ideas about father-rights, sometimes in a progressive voice, other times in a reactionary one" (48). Although a variety of men's issues organizations with a variety of orientations exists (Menzies 2007), this book focuses on antifeminist men's and fathers' rights groups because they have been the ones mounting legal attacks against protections for abused women in *Booth v. Hvass* and other cases.

Robert Menzies wrote that web-surfers who "tour the cyber-world of men's rights Web pages" are "quickly rewarded with a torrent of diatribes, invectives, atrocity tales, claims to entitlement, calls to arms, and prescriptions for change in the service of men, children, families, God, the past, the future, the nation, the planet, and all other things non-feminist" (2007, 65). Menzies observed that despite their hyperbolic "cacophony and bluster," antifeminist men's websites "represent an important context of material as well as cultural struggle for feminists, their adversaries, and their allies" (66). He catalogued prominent themes in antifeminist men's groups' complaints about feminism:

Feminism is defamatory, oppressive, and obsolete
Feminism threatens the nation
Feminism is an affront to Christianity
Feminism strikes at fatherhood and the family
Feminism monopolizes the media and throttles free speech
Feminism subverts men's rights and unleashes judicial bias
Feminism endangers men's health and safety. (2007, 72–85)

Booth v. Hvass takes up the latter four of these themes in its attack on Minnesota's domestic violence laws and services.

Lobbying on the part of antifeminist men's groups to change the subject from battered women to battered men is political, as were efforts to achieve recognition of woman battering as a social problem and crime rather than as simply a private matter (Schechter 1982). However, the politics of these movements could not be more different. In the 1970s, battered women fought to articulate their experiences of abuse and insist upon the right to be safe from violence in the context of social norms against intervention in men's violence against female intimate partners (Brownmiller 1975; Dobash and Dobash 1979; Gordon 1988; Schechter 1983). Threatened by these changes, contemporary antifeminists seek to reassert the patriarchal prerogative to define violence and delimit responses to it (Dragiewicz 2008). R. W. Connell has observed that men's groups have frequently drawn erroneous parallels between their organizing and that of such liberatory social movements as the women's and civil rights movements:

> "Men" as a group, and heterosexual men in particular, are not oppressed or disadvantaged. . . . men in general gain a patriarchal dividend. Hegemonic masculinity is not a stigmatized identity. Quite the opposite: the culture already honours it. Seeking the unity of "men" can only mean emphasizing the experiences and interests men have that separate them from women, rather than the interests they share with women that might lead towards social justice. (2000, 209)

Gwyneth Williams and Rhys Williams have also described how antifeminist men's and father's groups appropriate the liberal language of "equal rights" (1995). The civil rights movement attempted to promote individual liberties by eliminating discriminatory, segregationist laws. The liberal understanding was that formal legal equality would lead to substantive equality. However, Williams and Williams noted, later the rhetoric of the civil rights movement shifted from demands for the removal of barriers to rights claims. These two different conceptualizations of equal rights, "rights as liberties" and "rights as claims," can be applied to a variety of political goals (Williams and Williams 1995, 195–96).

Williams and Williams argued that the path of early liberal feminism was similar to the path of the civil rights movement. Where the civil rights movement called for a "colorblind" application of the law in response to explicitly discriminatory Jim Crow laws, liberal feminists promoted formal equality through "gender-neutrality" in an attempt to eliminate structural barriers to women's equality with men (1995, 196). Antifeminist groups later appropriated the language of gender neutrality to attack programs created to ameliorate the outcomes of gendered inequality (Fineman 1994; Menzies 2007; Walby 1990; Williams and Williams 1995).

Antifeminist men's rights groups have proliferated since the 1970s. During the same period, no-fault divorce spread nationwide, VAWA began to encourage the arrest and prosecution of batterers, and the federal Office of Child Support Enforcement began to encourage the collection of child support by withholding tax refunds, garnishing wages, denying passports, and requiring employers to register new hires with state child support collection agencies (Dragiewicz 2008). These developments shed some light on the main priorities of antifeminist men's groups, which revolve around ameliorating the impact of sanctions against woman abuse and the failure to pay child support (Dragiewicz 2008; Rosen, Dragiewicz, and Gibbs 2009).

Fathers' rights groups have enjoyed enhanced visibility since the 1990s, when the United States government began to provide funding through the National Fatherhood Initiative to promote heterosexual marriage (Catlett and Artis 2004; Garrett 2003; Rosen, Dragiewicz, and Gibbs 2009). The ubiquity of the internet has played a part in this increased visibility as well; many groups meet only on the web (Dragiewicz 2008; Menzies 2007). Fathers' rights groups in the United States appear to be overwhelmingly made up of white men who identify themselves as college-educated professionals (Crowley 2009).

Changing demographics including increasing rates of cohabitation and divorce, decreasing rates of marriage, later marriage, and decreasing remarriage among women have contributed to higher numbers of children living with unmarried mothers (Catlett and Artis 2004; Crowley 2009; Rosen, Dragiewicz, and Gibbs 2009). In combination with cuts to welfare programs to mothers with dependent children, these demographic shifts have led to a surge in demand for child support. Because men are more likely than women to remarry following divorce, they face the possibility of paying support for children even after remarriage regardless of the presence of additional children. All of these factors contributed to the emergence of fathers' rights groups (Crowley 2009; Dragiewicz 2008; Rosen, Dragiewicz, and Gibbs 2009; Williams and Williams 1995).

While the connection between child support and woman abuse may not be immediately apparent to outside observers, the two issues are central and intertwined for antifeminist men's and fathers' rights groups. In one interview study of fathers' rights group members, 97 of 158 respondents, or 61 percent, talked about domestic violence without being asked about it. In addition, about 25 percent, or 40 of the 158 men, specifically named the battered women's movement as their political opponent (Crowley 2009, 731). One interviewee, Gerard, stated,

> One of the other groups [that our fathers' rights group] battles with is the domestic violence group. Here in [our state] as well as in other places, anybody just has to pick up the phone and say, I fear for myself and child, and [the man is] guilty of domestic violence until [he proves himself] innocent. . . . The custodial parent [then] gets sole custody for two years and the non-

custodial parent will probably get supervised visitation at [his] expense. And that can range anywhere from $45 to $80 dollars an hour, which means [that these fathers] are not going to see their kids. (Crowley 2009, 736)

Gerard's complaint—that women who report violence are always believed and are rewarded for reporting with such incentives as sole custody and child support—is common to both antifeminist groups and batterers. Several of the men in the study explained their opposition to the battered women's movement as related to its efforts to prevent the reduction of child support payments. Ethan told an interviewer,

In this past year . . . a domestic violence group said that [its members] didn't want to change [child support or child custody law] because [its members] felt that less money would end up going to moms. So, on the surface, these groups seem like they are just promoting moms' rights, not children's rights, to enjoy money directly from their dads the way a married family would, I think. (Crowley 2009, 734)

The notion that child support helps mothers is also common among antifeminist fathers' rights groups. Jonathan, who claimed a judge gave his wife their house because of what he described as a "false" order for protection, shared a similar complaint:

You essentially lose your rights. . . . That was instrumental in my losing of my property rights because the judge noted that there was a restraining order applied for—even though it was investigated and dismissed—that was used by him to decide that the house should go to her because she might be inclined to seek another restraining order. . . . It seems all very well and good what [the battered women's movement is] trying to accomplish to protect women from violence. But what is really being accomplished is the ones who are using these laws are not the ones who are truly in jeopardy, because a piece of paper isn't very effective in protecting a woman from violence but it is very effective in establishing a firm upper hand in a divorce situation. (Crowley 2009, 735)

Jonathan asserted that his ex-wife made a "false allegation" of violence in order to secure a financial benefit, even though the court apparently deemed her report of abuse sufficiently credible to award her the house in a divorce settlement. Fathers' rights activists object to the protections available to battered women where they affect their own privileges, most often when they have either been subject to an order for protection or convicted on a domestic violence complaint, the cases in which child support or custody determination may take domestic violence into account.

While antifeminist fathers' rights groups are often identified with fringe or radical backlash perspectives and activities, their rhetoric overlaps considerably with mainstream journalism and scholarship (Boyd 2003; DeKeseredy and Dragiewicz 2007; Dragiewicz 2008; Flood 2010). Claims that domestic violence is sex-symmetrical are at the core of this confluence. The assimilation of the radical antifeminist ideas of fathers' rights groups into mainstream conversations and politics demands attention because, unlike women's violence against male intimate partners, men's violence against female intimate partners represents a disproportionate threat to women's lives, even after the end of an abusive relationship (Boyd 2003; Flood 2010; Girard 2009; Mann 2008).

The Social Ecology of Woman Abuse

Understanding violence as shaped by gender inequality is an idea gaining increasing acceptance around the world (World Health Organization 2002). However, confusion remains about what it means to assert that violence is gendered and what it means to say that patriarchy contributes to violence. This uncertainty is present even among some scholars who acknowledge the structural factors involved in violence and abuse. Despite suggestions that the United States is no longer "truly patriarchal" because "women's rights have finally been acknowledged after centuries of religion-based oppression" (Dutton 2006, ix), patriarchy continues to be central to woman abuse at all levels of the social ecology, and many of the sex differences in violence are symptomatic of patriarchal norms, practices, and institutions. Discussion of the rates of violence experienced and perpetrated by women and men cannot substitute for discussion of patriarchy and gender as contributing factors to violence.

Sylvia Walby has articulated the most comprehensive contemporary theory of patriarchy by defining it as "a system of social structures and practices in which men dominate, oppress, and exploit women" (1990, 20). Walby stressed the structural component of this definition because it clearly contradicts claims that patriarchy is rooted in biology and the idea that patriarchy means "every individual man is in a dominant position and every woman is in a subordinate one" (20).

To understand patriarchy and violence adequately their contributing and contextual factors must be integrated, a process perhaps best accom-

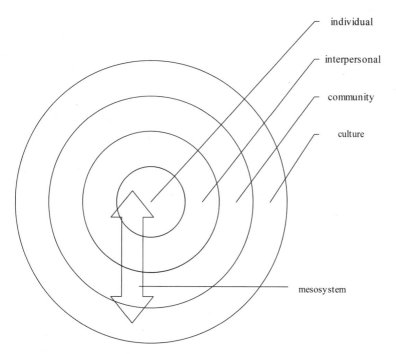

individual

interpersonal

community

culture

mesosystem

1.1 Ecological Model for Violence

plished by using an ecological model to analyze them. Building upon Urie Bronfenbrenner's theory of human development (1979; 1986), ecological theories of woman abuse consider the interaction of multiple systems in the production of violence (Carlson 1984; Edleson and Tolman 1992; Heise 1998). The World Health Organization's ecological model of violence (2002) is made up of a series of concentric rings representing different levels of social organization.

At the center of the ecological model is the individual. Survivors, abusers, and all of the people who interact with them are situated in a system of interacting contexts that comprise their social environment.

The interpersonal level—the immediate interpersonal contexts or settings in which an individual is directly engaged—is the next level of the social ecology. These contexts include a person's relationships and direct interactions with family, intimate partners, friends, coworkers, neighbors, police, the courts, and others (Edleson and Tolman 1992). The interpersonal level describes both a person's interactions with others and their effects.

The next level of the social ecology, the community, refers to larger contexts and interactions in which individuals do not engage directly but that still exert a cumulative, indirect effect on them. Jeffrey Edleson and Richard Tolman (1992) have noted that for male batterers, the community level includes the interpersonal and organizational contexts that affect abusive men indirectly, such as the coordination of community responses to violence and abuse (14). The community includes such factors as media coverage of violence and abuse; federal legislation, such as VAWA; local laws and policies; and court practices.

Bronfenbrenner described the cultural context, the next level of social ecology, as the set of ideological and structural "blueprints" for a particular culture (1979). These blueprints are pervasive and normative. However, although cultural factors may be hegemonic, they are not monolithic. Even dominant cultural norms are contested. In addition, culture changes over time in response to shifting social imperatives.

In addition to these levels, the chronosystem refers to temporal context, including change over time and personal, community, and cultural history (Bronfenbrenner 1979, 1986). How individuals and communities talk and think about violence against women changes over time in ways that shape the meaning of experiences and the material realities that are produced by them (Edleson and Tolman 1992).

Finally, the mesosystem describes the interaction between the other levels of the social ecology. In one sense, the mesosystem is the most important part of the ecological model because it describes the cumulative interaction of all of the other levels upon a person. The mesosystem describes an individual's entire experience in context; it captures, for example, the interaction between an individual's personal history of abuse, experienced in the context of a specific relationship, in which the individual has access to particular resources in a community and cultural context that shapes his or her interpretation of events and perception of available responses (Bronfenbrenner 1979, 1986; Edleson and Tolman 1992).

The ecological framework can be used to understand many forms of human behaviour, including multiple forms of violence, and can point to structural similarities and differences between them. Ecological models for violence against intimates thus reinforce critical theories by underscoring the importance of multiple, structural, and interpersonal factors in social phenomena. The integrated ecological framework helps to explain why some men become violent and others do not as well as why men are more violent than women in general (Heise 1998). It also illustrates how a multitude of factors must be considered if we are to understand the meaning and impact of individual violent acts (Dasgupta 2002).

As Allan Johnson argued, one hallmark of patriarchy is that women's perspectives are marginalized and men's interests are equated with the general public interest (2005, 157). Johnson observed that men normally occupy the unmarked "generic" standard for humanity, while women are marked as "other" (155). While men's interests and perspectives are often taken as neutral, women's are marked as biased. One example of patriarchy is the claim that violence is a "human issue" rather than a "gender issue" (McNeely and Mann 1990; Pizzey 2006). While women's *and* men's experiences are profoundly gendered, women's nondominant status means that the word "gender" is often used as code for "woman." In everyday discourse, when men are implicitly at the center, gender is not mentioned. The idea that human issues and gender issues are mutually exclusive is instructive. In effect, including gender means including women. The implication of insisting that domestic violence is a human rather than a gender issue is that paying attention to gender means paying attention to women. In the context of patriarchal hegemony, focusing attention on women's particular experiences and needs is unwarranted, abnormal, and intolerable. Objections to the recognition of gender as a factor in social life are also objections to the recognition of women and their experiences. Accordingly, contemporary efforts to enforce gender-blindness in areas where gender is pertinent essentially function as objections to the prioritization of women's experiences.

Despite the complaints of antifeminists, masculinity and maleness are normally implicit rather than explicit in discussions about men's violence against women. We frequently talk of woman abuse, wife beating, or violence against women without explicitly naming men as the perpetrators. Antifeminist activists object even to this implicit recognition of men's disproportionate violence against women. They simultaneously insist that we stop acknowledging men's disproportionate violence against women (which they appear to believe results in a harm to men that outweighs the harm from men's violence against women) and talk more about women's violence against men (which they suggest circumvents the need for critical consideration of patriarchy).

Miranda Kaye and Julia Tolmie have observed that in calls for gender neutrality and other demands for formal equality "gender equality arguments are generally couched as arguments that men and women should be equally treated according to standards developed from the life experiences of men, when in fact they are differently situated" (1998, 166). Formal equality, or treating dissimilarly situated people similarly, perpetuates and exacerbates existing inequalities (Kaye and Tolmie 1998, 166). Calls for gender-blind approaches to violence are essentially demands that we become blind to women's particular experiences of violence. Antifeminist complaints about service providers that assist men *and* recognize the contribution of patriarchy to violence make this clear. It is not enough for agencies created to assist battered women also to serve men. Antifeminists also demand that battered women's advocates stop discussing patriarchy and other forms of gender-based privilege and oppression. What groups like those sponsoring *Booth v. Hvass* express as "rights" are actually demands for the enforcement of patriarchal privilege. What they articulate as a request for equal protection is a request to have men's experiences reasserted as definitive in this exceptional location where women's credibility is sometimes recognized.

Thus, it was no accident that *Booth v. Hvass* targeted shelters for battered women. Likewise, it is no surprise that orders for protection were a secondary target of the lawsuit. Walby (1990) identified shelters and orders for protection (OFP) as two key legal "interventions against male violence":

> Firstly, feminists have organized to provide support services for women who have suffered male violence, especially in establishing refuges for battered women to escape to. . . . These forms of political intervention started as self-help agencies in which feminists drew upon their own resources to establish new feminist institutions, and only later did many of them receive partial funding from the state, often at a local level. (147)

Secondly, Walby pointed to "attempts to make changes in the way the state responds to women's complaints of violence" (147). While it is still rare for men to be subjected to criminal penalties for violence against female intimates, orders for protection create a paper trail that makes negative consequences more likely in the future. Once they are imposed, protective orders define further abusive behavior as a crime. To some batterers and their allies, the availability and enforcement of protective orders and other legal remedies for violence against intimates constitute feminist domination of the state (Dragiewicz 2008). In a speech to the R-KIDS Legal Action Committee (one of the fathers' rights groups involved with *Booth v. Hvass*) *Booth* plaintiff Steven Blake said,

Many of our members have been ordered from their homes by armed agents of the state; given 30 minutes to collect a few belongings and then leave— often with no provision of where they are to go or even how to get there. (Where have we heard of this happening before?)

Many of our members have suddenly been denied access to their children, often based on false or wildly exaggerated claims of "domestic abuse."... A family court system that seems to forget that women can be angry, vindictive, vengeful, cruel and that they can be willing to lie in order to access that most powerful weapon—the women center advocate, and to misuse the domestic protection laws and have the State of Minnesota wield the club with which they get their revenge. A family court system that treats flouting of court orders by mothers, especially denial of visitation, sharing of records and information or phone contact with children, as of little consequence, yet vigorously enforces (with police and with jail) violations of OFP (orders for protection, ed.) or Child Support Orders. (R-KIDS 1999)

While Blake's claims raise many questions about the nature of group members' interactions with the state (and their ex-wives), they reveal a depth of entitlement to patriarchal privilege that often goes unspoken. When men lose the prerogative to define what constitutes violence and abuse against women, some men experience this as a violation of their rights as men, especially when "armed agents of the state" apply the law to the benefit of women. The idea that resources useful to women are evidence of feminist control of the state is repeated on other antifeminist websites. One antifeminist blog quoted the plaintiff in an unsuccessful equal protection lawsuit against Columbia University as having stated, "When it comes to Men's Rights, judges act with an arrogance of power, ignorance of the law, and fear of the Feminists" (Men's Rights Blog 2009).

Readers might ask why groups that are ostensibly concerned about men's issues have focused on women's violence, which comprises a tiny portion of the violence men experience. Violence is primarily a men's issue, because they use it most often and are victimized most often. However, the battered women's movement brought attention to the forms of violence women most commonly experience, those perpetrated by male intimates. As a result, in this one area, the formally neutral term "domestic violence" was typified as men's violence against women. Antifeminists then portrayed those who acknowledged this form of violence as biased special-interest groups. As the *Booth* plaintiffs put it,

The problem of domestic violence was taken out of the closet twenty-five years ago by screaming demagogues who had no interest in solving problems, but a cunning desire to stir up destructive outrage, and thereby seize power, as illustrated so strikingly by the speeches in favour of the "bill for an act relating to women" on May 20, 1977, in the Minnesota House of Representatives. Those who have dared here to parrot the egregious bigotry there expressed, as if it were the wisdom of statesmen, have spoken rashly and should reconsider what they have said. (Plaintiffs' omnibus answer to amici curiae 2001, 7)

Interesting / irony

In a related example, Allan Johnson observed, "In general, women are made invisible when they do something that might raise their status. . . . Men, however, are often made invisible when their behavior is socially undesirable and might raise questions about the appropriateness of male privilege" (2005, 155). He continued, "On those rare occasions when someone mentions statistics on male violence and suggests this might be a problem worth looking at, the response is yawning impatience ('Oh, this again?') or, more likely, a torrent of objections to the male-bashing straw man defense: 'You're accusing all men of being murderers and rapists!'" (156). In fact, much of the contemporary rhetoric about sex symmetry in violence against intimates emulates male batterers' narratives about their violence. Recognizing this similarity is important because abuser accounts reflect ways of thinking that justify abusers' continued abuse of their partners and draw upon those mainstream discourses about women, men, and families that indirectly support abusers in efforts to retain control over their partners (Bancroft 2002).

Martin Schwartz and Walter DeKeseredy (1993) described the way that social problems are addressed in academia and the press through a process of "typification" that selectively translates research and anecdotal evidence into "typical" cases that guide legislation, "common sense" knowledge, and programs and services. Examining how male batterers frame their violence as not violent, not their fault, and not their responsibility—how batterers typify their violence—makes it possible to understand better the ways of thinking that engender men's violence against women. Regardless of its veracity, the typification of violence against intimates as sex-symmetrical in general contributes to the conceptualization of violence as mutual in specific, individual relationships. Significantly, such understandings of violence are not only characteristic of batterers' accounts. Many battered women who are not yet able to end the relationship permanently employ victim-blaming and batterer-exonerating narratives that allow them survive in the situation until they are able to leave (Wood 2001). The ubiquity of discourses that mimic those of batterers (and survivors who are not yet able to leave) impedes the affirmation of other ways of thinking about violence. Squeezed out by these abuse-enabling accounts are counterstories, including the perspectives of survivors who have left their abusers and of the majority of women and men who do not coercively control their partners.

It is important to pay attention to the way that violence is discussed in *Booth v. Hvass* and other contexts because of the real-world consequences of typifying violence in ways that mimic or challenge batterers. While men can be victims of intimate violence and women can be perpetrators, there are pervasive and significant sex and gender differences in the kinds of violence they are likely to use and experience. Accounting for sex and gender is therefore essential to understanding violence against women *and* men (Johnson and Ferraro 2000; Osthoff et al. 2002).

2 | Booth v. Hvass

> The purpose of this suit is to cut off the main source of public money
> which fuels sexist bias against men in our family court system.
> —*Legal Action Committee 2001b*

> The Legal Action Committee has brought together the resources to
> initiate a federal lawsuit to remove this discriminatory legislation from
> Minnesota law and deny Battered Women Shelters [*sic*] this public
> funding for an obviously private and destructive purpose.
> —*Legal Action Committee 2001a*

The R-KIDS Legal Action Committee, the Men's Defense Association,
and the National Coalition of Free Men, Twin Cities Chapter, filed the
Booth v. Hvass case in October 2000 in the United States District Court
for the State of Minnesota. The lawsuit attempted to eliminate the mechanism for the disbursement of state funding to battered women's shelters
and other agencies serving what Minnesota law refers to as "battered
women and other victims of domestic abuse." *Booth v. Hvass* also sought
to effect a broader fundamental change in contemporary understandings
of violence and abuse. The case characterized discourses about and services for battered women as discriminatory. The plaintiffs argued that
the state discriminated against men when service providers acknowledged
that sex and gender differences were involved in woman battering and
other forms of domestic abuse. *Booth v. Hvass* joined other antifeminist
efforts to reclaim patriarchal authority and the rhetorical space won by
women over the past fifty years by enforcing a gender-blind understanding of a highly gendered social problem (Dragiewicz 2008). *Booth v. Hvass*
shows how symbolic battles over language and representation relate to
concerns as concrete as the allocation of resources and as abstract as cultural norms for social life. In particular, the case shows how discourses on
violence and abuse are a site of conflict over gender.

Booth's amended complaint included twenty-three sections which sought to

establish the plaintiffs' standing to sue;

confirm the jurisdiction of the court to hear the case;

argue the unconstitutionality of the statutes the plaintiffs referred to as the "Minnesota Battered Women's Act";

enumerate the specific pieces of legislation to which the suit refers;

articulate the reasons for targeting the selected defendants;

list a series of complaints about the legislation in question;

argue about the alleged effects of the legislation;

assert that women are as violent as or more violent than men;

contend that "female violence is, in any event, a major social problem";

provide citations to support claims about sex symmetry in intimate-partner violence; and

demand that the current legislation be declared "null and void as if never passed, insofar as it funds battered women's shelters certified and approved under the act" in order to prevent any further state funding of services for battered women and other victims of domestic abuse in Minnesota. (Amended complaint 2000)

The plaintiffs sued officials including the Commissioners of Correction, Human Services, Public Safety, and Children, Families, and Learning for the state of Minnesota. After attempting to establish the plaintiffs' right to sue as state taxpayers, *Booth* argued that men were denied domestic violence services in the state. The plaintiffs asserted that targeting services to battered women was discriminatory because men are just as likely as women to be victims of domestic violence. *Booth* also charged that the rhetoric disseminated by recipients of state antiviolence funds created prejudice against all men as members of a sex class (Amended complaint 2000, 5).

The plaintiffs argued that "the legislative history of this Act decisively proves that it was intended on bigoted assumptions to discriminate against men in favor of women" (Plaintiffs' omnibus answer to amici curiae 2001, 14). The plaintiffs argued that this discrimination arose because Minnesota domestic violence laws had been inspired by "defamatory falsehoods about men in general" (Amended complaint 2000, 3). Minnesota's shelter funding was established based on the unmet needs of battered women, which the *Booth* plaintiffs asserted were "ideological tripe and contrivances" (Plaintiffs' omnibus answer to amici curiae 2001, 7).

Thus, the plaintiffs argued, state funding for services should be abolished, and the research the state relied upon to justify the creation of the shelters should be disregarded in favor of a new approach to intimate partner violence that would exclude gender and treat violence as a disease in which women and men are mutually implicated. Significantly, the desired outcome of the case was not more services for men but the elimination of all state-funded domestic violence services, including those the plaintiffs knew helped men.[1]

The United States District Court for the State of Minnesota dismissed *Booth v. Hvass* with prejudice on August 13, 2001, based on its determination that the *Booth* plaintiffs lacked standing to pursue their case. Standing refers to the fact that none of the men had been harmed by the legislation in question. The men had protested the allocation of state dollars as taxpayers, but the court deemed protest on this basis illegitimate. Seeking to have both their standing to sue and the merits (or underlying issues) of the case considered on appeal, all but one of the *Booth* plaintiffs appealed the dismissal in October 2001. The United States Court of Appeals for the Eighth Circuit affirmed the decision of the lower court in September 2002 based on the appellants' lack of standing to bring the suit. The court commented that because state spending did not facilitate discrimination against the appellants, they had not suffered injury under the equal protection clause (*Booth v. Hvass* 2002). In 2003, the *Booth* appellants petitioned to have the Supreme Court of the United States review their case, but the petition was denied (*Booth v. Hvass* 2003).

The plaintiffs in *Booth v. Hvass* actively encouraged others to bring similar lawsuits. They wrote, "Our argument may be pursued in any state that is granted funds under the VAWA for a purpose here shown to be ineffective and unlawful. We can direct a request for research assistance to our resources, or use the record of our case to map an investigative coarse [*sic*]" (Legal Action Committee 2001a).

While the potential harm of eliminating funding for services as *Booth v. Hvass* advocated was averted because the case was dismissed, antifeminist men's groups have promoted and assisted subsequent lawsuits in other states.[2] So far, one equal protection lawsuit against shelters in California has been partially successful. In *Woods v. Horton* (2008), the court's decision directed that shelter funding under California's Health and Safety Code § 124250 and Penal Code § 13823.15 be allocated without regard for gender because male and female victims exist. The decision also stated, "In reforming the statutes that provide funding for domestic violence programs to be gender-neutral, the court does not require that such programs offer identical services to men and women. Given the noted disparity in the number of women needing services and the greater severity of their injuries, it may be appropriate to provide more and different services to battered women and their children" (*Woods v. Horton* 2008).

In practice this wording has shielded California shelters, because the shelters already offered services to men such as counseling, referrals, and hotel vouchers even if some emergency residential shelter facilities are designated for women and children.[3] To date, none of the equal protection lawsuits has succeeded in eliminating funding for shelters, preventing the enforcement of domestic violence laws, or imposing a gender-blind conception of violence as *Booth v. Hvass* set out to do.

However, *Booth v. Hvass* incorporated several of the major elements common to current attacks by antifeminist men's groups on legislation, services, and policies aiding battered women in the United States, Australia, Canada, and the United Kingdom (Chunn, Boyd, and Lessard 2007; Collier and Sheldon 2006; DeKeseredy 1999; DeKeseredy and Dragiewicz 2007; Dragiewicz 2008; Dragiewicz and Lindgren 2009; Flood 1999, 2010; Girard 2009; Kaye and Tolmie 1998; Mann 2008; Rosen, Dragiewicz, and Gibbs 2009). Accordingly, the lawsuit is useful as a case study of the arguments and evidence used in such attacks and their resonance in the United States and other locations. The case's ongoing relevance stems from the fact that the claims presented in the complaint are not unique but instead are borrowed from antifeminist discourses circulating in other contexts.

Why Equal Protection Arguments Matter

The claims that domestic violence is not a gender issue and that women are just as violent as men are repeated frequently in the media, often in the context of antifeminist activism. This repetition occurs despite unmistakable evidence that violence against intimates is both profoundly gendered and sex asymmetrical. The repetition of symmetry claims needs to be addressed because it will likely shape further efforts to undermine antiviolence law and policy. The hazard is that gender-blind notions of violence and abuse will result in a return to the putatively gender-neutral, privatized approach to violence that preceded the battered women's movement. Prior to feminist activism in the area of violence against women there were no shelters for battered women (Martin 1981), existing laws against assault were often not enforced when perpetrators were men and victims were their female intimate partners (Buzawa and Buzawa 1996), and there was no such crime as marital rape (Finkelhor and Yllö 1985). Concern about the implications of reversing feminist activism on violence against women is underscored by the ways that contemporary antifeminist claims affirm batterer narratives.

The most serious implication of the arguments presented in *Booth v. Hvass* is that they misrepresent the research in order to make the claim that violence is sex-symmetrical. These distortions are not merely of theoretical concern, given that the ways that we understand and talk about violence have serious ramifications for preventing it, intervening against it, or otherwise responding to it. Despite protestations about the "politicization" of violence against women, all ways of understanding the problem have political and practical implications that must be acknowledged. The specific and disturbing implications of the sex-symmetry claims promoted in and around *Booth v. Hvass* become very clear when we look at how these claims fit into and function in other discourses.

As feminist and critical scholars assert, efforts to create and validate knowledge are always political. Competing perspectives legitimate different kinds of power. While the struggle over meaning occurs across many discourses, law is one of the few areas where hegemonic meanings are actually enforced. In the case of the law and violence against intimates, hegemonic meanings determine what is a crime and what is not.

Violence against women was originally identified as a social problem by feminists and is one of the most visible areas in which feminist concepts have been institutionalized in the United States (Brooks 1997). As a result of their roots in feminist activism, efforts to address violence against women are a controversial area of scholarship and law despite widespread public condemnation of such violence. *Booth* saw legislation and services targeting domestic violence as "destructive" and regarded both efforts to meet demand for emergency housing for battered women and the availability of protective orders as promoting "sexist bias against men." The plaintiffs in *Booth v. Hvass* claimed that "domestic violence is a problem shared by men and women, the same as alcoholism is a problem shared by men and women" (Plaintiffs' omnibus answer to motions of the defendants 2001, 7). *Booth* also argued,

> The cumulative effect of the said programs and spending under and through the Battered Women's Act is the creation of a prejudicial atmosphere against men in general before the judiciary, especially the family

courts, of the State of Minnesota, depriving them, because they are men, of equal and impartial justice under law, and creating a dangerous situation in which they may be evicted from their homes and deprived of custodial and parental rights to their children on ex parte application without notice and hearing. (Amended complaint 2000, 5)

At the same time that they asserted concern about violence against women was overblown, the *Booth* plaintiffs alleged that feminists affiliated with shelters encouraged women to make false reports and that the existence of an epidemic of husband battering was "in any event, a major social problem" (Amended complaint 2000, 6). *Booth* presented convoluted and contradictory claims in order to achieve this framing of domestic violence.

Resistance to creating and enforcing laws addressing violence against intimates has historically included claims that minimize violence against women by suggesting that it is not really a significant problem but has instead been "hyped" by feminists for monetary or personal gain (Dunn 1994; Hoff Sommers 1994). While antifeminists claim that attention to men's violence against women is exaggerated, they also frequently claim that there is a hidden epidemic of husband battering which constitutes a serious social problem requiring increased funding and attention similar to that granted to wife battering (Steinmetz 1977–78). Repetition of these claims is at the core of the *Booth* complaint.

Significantly, *Booth v. Hvass* does not explain why the claim that women are as violent as men should lead to the conclusion that no state funds should be spent on services for women or men. The complaint pays no attention to male victims of violence aside from the argument that their existence renders women's and men's experiences of violence similar. *Booth v. Hvass* proposes no assistance to male victims. In fact, the only place the victimization of men is addressed in the context of Minnesota laws and services is in the discussion of men as the putative victims of prejudice in the criminal and family courts when they have been reported, arrested, or evicted for perpetrating violence.

The Equal Protection Claim

Booth's legal claim is that Minnesota's domestic violence laws are unconstitutional because they violate the equal protection clause of the Fourteenth Amendment by allegedly providing services and shelter to battered women and denying them to battered men (*Booth v. Hvass* 2000).[4] Understanding the nature of the equal protection clause and the case law that guides its interpretation is critical to understanding this case and others based on equal protection claims. The Fourteenth Amendment to the Constitution of the United States, which was ratified in 1868, established the rights of citizenship for some African American men in the United States, including the right to vote. Its broad language guaranteeing "the privileges or immunities of citizens of the United States," rights to due process, and equal protection of the law provided the foundation for contemporary civil rights in America (Dragiewicz and Lindgren 2009; Garrett 2003; U.S. Constitution Amendment XIV, §1; Zick 2000/2001).

Section 1 of the equal protection clause stipulates that no state may "deny any person within its jurisdiction the equal protection of the laws." *Booth* argued that failing to treat women and men identically by housing men in the same shelters that house abused women violates this guarantee.[5] However, legal precedent has established that equal protection does not require "things which are different in fact or opinion to be treated in law as though they were the same" (*Tigner v. Texas* 1980). Supreme Court decisions have also determined that the existence of group-based classifications is not necessarily prohibited. The equal protection clause prohibits treating *similarly situated* individuals differently based on their class affiliation alone (Dragiewicz and Lindgren 2009; Garrett 2003). Court decisions affirm that "statutes create many classifications which do not deny Equal Protection; it is only 'invidious discrimination' which offends the Constitution" (*Ferguson v. Skrupa* 1963). Thus, discriminating *between* groups for legitimate governmental purposes is often allowable, while discriminating *against* individuals based on group affiliations is often not permitted.[6]

The standards for scrutinizing group-based classifications differ according to the class or category in question. There are three different standards for scrutiny. The lowest form of scrutiny is "rational basis," which is applied to most "non-suspect" group-based classifications (Zick 2000/2001). For example, in *FCC v. Beach Communications Inc.* (1993) the opinion of the Supreme Court of the United States stated,

> In areas of social and economic policy, a statutory classification that neither proceeds along suspect lines nor infringes fundamental constitutional rights must be upheld against Equal Protection challenge if any reasonably conceivable state of facts could provide a rational basis for the classification.

This level of scrutiny allows many classifications to stand because they need only be made on some rational basis.

An intermediate level of scrutiny is applied to gender[7] classifications at the federal level and in most states. Gender-based classifications are currently considered quasi-suspect and are thus subject to "heightened" or "intermediate" scrutiny (National Women's Law Center 2001). The intermediate standard of scrutiny means that in order for "gender-based classifications to withstand constitutional challenge under the Equal Protection clause of the Fourteenth Amendment, classifications by gender must serve important governmental objectives and must be substantially related to achievement of those objectives" (*Craig v. Boren* 1976).

Race-based classifications are subject to a third standard of review, "strict scrutiny." For example, as the court stated in *Korematsu v. United States* (1944),

> It should be noted, to begin with, that all legal restrictions which curtail the civil rights of a single racial group are immediately suspect. That is not to say that all such restrictions are unconstitutional. It is to say that courts must subject them to the most rigid scrutiny.

The highest standard of scrutiny means that most race-based classifications are not deemed legitimate and are ultimately not upheld. Legal scholars have noted that the standards for scrutiny are fluid, and interpretation is contingent on the composition of the court and changing social norms over time (Garrett 2003; Zick 2000/2001).

Where sex or gender differences are concerned, the justification for drawing a distinction must be "based upon a real difference between the classes, such that the different treatment is justified under the circumstances being addressed by the government" (Garrett 2003, 347). Distinctions must not rely on stereotypes about women and men but should reflect actual circumstances. In other words, sex-based classifications are only legitimate if they are applied to an area in which women and men are differently situated that is also closely related to a government objective. For example, it is illegal to bar women from employment based on a gender-based assumption about women's interest in working in a certain field, but it is legal to acknowledge real differences such as the fact that women give birth and men do not by affording maternity leave to women and not to men. Accordingly, the burden of the plaintiffs in *Booth v. Hvass* was to show that women and men are similarly situated with regard to domestic violence. Thus, *Booth* claims, "The repetitious conclusion of [studies on violence against intimates] is that, globally speaking, men and women are both guilty of about equal rates of domestic violence" (Appellants' reply to amici curiae, 2). Because such claims are popular with a variety of antifeminist commentators (Leo 1994; McElroy 1995; McNeely and Robinson Simpson 1987, 1988; Young 1994), an analysis of the claims, evidence, and demands presented in *Booth v. Hvass* is highly relevant to other discourses and contexts.

Claims and Evidence

All of the substantive claims made in *Booth v. Hvass* relied upon the presumption of sex symmetry in domestic violence. In their complaint, the *Booth* plaintiffs objected to the existence of shelter services for battered women, protested recognition of sex and gender differences in domestic violence, and argued that the original Minnesota legislation was intended to discriminate against men in favor of women, not to address domestic violence. All of these claims are based upon the primary insistence that women and men are similarly (symmetrically) situated with regard to domestic violence.

As evidence to support their complaints, *Booth* provided a small collection of documents. To illustrate that some domestic violence materials and services acknowledge sex and gender differences, they cited a handout, a brochure, and a booklet. To allege that Minnesota's original domestic violence legislation was intended to discriminate against men, they pointed to a partial transcript from a 1977 discussion in the Minnesota House of Representatives. To argue that women and men were similarly situated with regard to domestic violence, they used as evidence a chapter from an anthology and an annotated bibliography. However, when read in their entirety and placed in their historical, political, and scholarly context, each of these documents provides evidence that refutes the assertion of sex symmetry in domestic violence.

The first exhibit introduced by *Booth* was a handout. The amended complaint described it in these terms:

> An illustration of such sexist hate literature against men, funded under and through the Battered Women's Act, is a notorious circular, commonly call [*sic*] the "Power and Control Wheel" and published by the so-called "Domestic Abuse Intervention Project" in the City of Duluth. (Amended complaint, 4–5)

The Duluth Domestic Abuse Intervention Project created the power and control wheel (see fig. 2.1) to represent graphically some of the tactics commonly reported by heterosexual women who are survivors of violence perpetrated by male intimate partners (Pence and Paymar 1993). The power and control wheel lists these forms of abuse:

using coercion and threats
using intimidation
using emotional abuse
using isolation
minimizing, denying, and blaming
using children
using male privilege
using economic abuse

The wheel lists several examples under each category. For example, the category "using coercion and threats" includes "making and/or carrying out threats to do something to hurt her; threatening to leave her, to commit suicide, to report her to welfare; making her drop charges; making her do illegal things." The category "using intimidation" includes "making her afraid by using looks, actions, gestures; smashing things; destroying her property; abusing pets; displaying weapons" (Pence and Paymar 1993). *Booth* does not explain why the plaintiffs view this handout as "notorious," as "sexist hate literature against men," or as otherwise objectionable. The plaintiffs only asserted that the Domestic Abuse Intervention Project was

> listed in a legal manual urging use of orders for protection and like orders mainly against men, and entitled Getting Court Orders for Protection from Abuse and Harassment, Minnesota Legal Services Coalition, St. Paul, 3rd edition 1998, p. 43, as a battered women's shelter now in business in the State of Minnesota. The said manual is expressly premised on the notion, unsubstantiated by any empirical data gathered by qualified scholars in peer-reviewed journals, that all or nearly all—i.e., "over 95%" of—domestic violence is inflicted by men upon women. (Amended complaint 2000, 4)

Although this line of argument is difficult to follow, it appears to suggest that shelters should not circulate materials that acknowledge the gendered nature of woman abuse or the sex differences in violence perpetrated against intimates. The *Booth* plaintiffs rejected the cited claim that most domestic violence is perpetrated by men against women and the fact that more men than women are the subjects of orders for protection.

2.1 The Power and Control Wheel. *Courtesy of the Domestic Abuse Intervention Project.*

They also objected to the existence of the power and control wheel, apparently because it used gendered language and referred to abusive tactics. Contrary to the *Booth* plaintiffs' account of the origins of such tools in hysteria and ideology, the power and control wheel is based on research. Ellen Pence and Michael Paymar have described how and why the diagram was created:

> In 1984, based on group interviews with women attending educational classes offered by the Duluth battered women's shelter, we began developing a framework for describing the behavior of men who physically and

emotionally abuse their partners. Many of the women criticized theories that described battering as cyclical rather than as a constant force in their relationship; that attributed the violence to men's inability to cope with stress; and that failed to acknowledge fully the intention of batterers to gain control over their partners' actions, thoughts and feelings. Challenging the assumptions about why women stay with men who beat them, more than 200 battered women . . . designed the Power and Control Wheel, which depicts the primary abusive behaviors experienced by women living with men who batter. (1993, 2; internal citation omitted)

In this context, it is clear that a demand to remove gender from such educational tools as the power and control wheel would not render the tool "gender neutral." Instead, it would silence the voices of battered women and distort the realities of their experiences. In other words, the derivative versions of the power and control wheel that censor gendered language are based on speculation and ideology; the original tool is not. Furthermore, Pence and Paymar's account of why the battered women were dissatisfied with earlier theories about the nature of domestic violence points to the victim-blaming cultural context as well as practitioners' and scholars' unwillingness to describe the intentional nature of men's violence and abuse against women accurately.

Booth next complains,

The said battered women's shelters, funded under and through the Minnesota Battered Women's Act, also bring political pressure to bear on public officers of the State of Minnesota to publish fanatical, irrational, hysterical, sexist literature which maliciously and falsely defames and seeks to generate social and political hatred against men in general, portraying them as the basic cause of all domestic violence and associated acts of cruelty in American society. (Amended complaint 2000, 4)

The *Booth* plaintiffs cited a booklet titled *Confronting Domestic Violence* published in 2000 by the Dakota County, Minnesota, Attorney's Office, as an example of this literature (Amended complaint 2000, 5) but did not explain what they disliked about it. The handout defines domestic violence according to the Minnesota statutes as physical violence, restraint, sexual abuse, and threats where the perpetrator and victim "are current or former spouses; have or have had an intimate relationship, have a child together, or unborn child together, are related by blood or marriage" or "are family members residing in the same household"

(Dakota County Attorney's Office 2000, 1). On the same opening page the handout explains that domestic violence can happen in any group (same sex/opposite sex, rural/urban, rich/poor) and that 95 percent of domestic violence is against women. Finally, text on this first page explains that domestic violence happens because it is effective, allowing one partner to "dominate and control their relationships with their partners" in order to get what they want, and that a batterer typically believes that "he/she is entitled to the victim's obedience and service."

The second page of *Confronting Domestic Violence* describes some common batterer characteristics. The section titled, "Who is a 'typical' batterer?" includes statements such as, "Many batterers are not violent in other relationships, such as at work or with friends," "Many abusers have a rigid, traditional view of sex roles and parenting," and "Battering is a learned behavior, not a mental illness." Ten of the twelve statements on this page are worded in a gender-neutral manner. The first gendered statement reads, "A victim of domestic violence may distance herself from family or friends, fearing that they will discover the violence and blame her for it." The second states, "In the United States, approximately 30% of the women murdered are killed by their husbands, ex-husbands, or boyfriends."

Page 3 of the booklet describes "the nature of domestic violence," states that "the vast majority of victims are women," and lists some reasons why women are vulnerable to domestic violence, among them feeling obligated to keep the family together and the fact that women's financial situation often worsens after divorce. This third page also points out that the risk of homicide or injury increases for women at the point of separation from the batterer.

The handout's fourth page, titled, "How does domestic violence affect children?" describes the relationship between child abuse and domestic violence as well as the emotional and physical risks to children who witness abuse. Domestic violence, the text states, provokes fear in children, puts older children at risk of being harmed while trying to intervene in the violence, and potentially increases their risk of becoming involved in violent relationships later in life. On the fifth page, a section titled "Spankey gets earplugs" reproduces a child's story about a boy who stole money from his mother's purse to buy earplugs which he then wore everywhere he went. When the boy's friend asked him why he was wearing earplugs, Spankey said, "I don't want to hear my mom fight with my dad. I'm wearing them till they get a divorce."

Page 6, titled "How domestic violence affects the community," explains how domestic violence involves costs to the community—funding for social services, police and criminal justice expenses, and the increased need for medical care—beyond those directly involved in the abusive relationship. On page 7, a "message for parents" lists signs for parents to look for in their teens' dating relationships, as well as actions they can take if they notice abusive behavior. The text asks,

Is your teen's friend:

- Jealous and possessive?
- Bossy, gives orders, makes all the decisions?
- Scary; threatens, owns, or uses weapons?
- Violent; has a history of fighting, loses temper quickly, brags about mistreating others?

Should parents identify such behaviours, page seven advises parents to, among other things, "call an advocate at a battered women's program. Become informed. Lend a sympathetic ear. Talk to your teen about danger. Develop a safety plan."

The last three pages of the booklet focus on resources available to survivors of violence. The eighth page of the booklet summarizes relevant Minnesota laws and lists the criminal offenses related to domestic violence. Text on page 9, titled "Orders for Protection," explains what OFP are and lists some of the conditions they might establish; for example, an OFP might demand that an abuser "stop abusive conduct; stay away from the victim, the victim's home, work place, the victim's children or other family members." Page 9 of the handout lists the penalties for violation of OFPs, instructions for how to obtain an OFP, and information about other services battered women's programs offer. Page 10, the final page of the booklet, lists phone numbers for "battered women's programs," "police/law enforcement," and "other emergency or information numbers" (Dakota County Attorney's Office 2000). Overall, the booklet includes information about the state's gender-neutral laws and resources, includes information about warning signs that apply equally to women and men, and acknowledges some of the specific factors disproportionately affecting battered women. The parts of the booklet acknowledging women's disproportionate risk of being abused by male partners, being financially entrapped in abusive relationships, and being killed upon separation from an abuser relative to men were presumably the target of *Booth*'s objections.

Following their discussion of *Confronting Domestic Violence*, the *Booth* plaintiffs cited their third exhibit, a partial transcript from a House of Representatives debate that apparently took place on May 20, 1977. According to the complaint, the debate centered on

> a bill for an act relating to women, establishing pilot programs to provide emergency shelter and support services to battered women, providing funds to establish community education programs about battered women, providing for data collection, waiving certain general assistance eligibility requirements for battered women, appropriating money, and amending Minnesota Statutes 1976, Section 256D.05, by adding a subdivision. (Amended complaint 2000, 5)

The plaintiffs argued that the transcript showed that the "main supporter of the bill directed swelling demagogic and propagandist oratory against men as the culprits in all domestic violence in American [society and ridiculed] the suggestion by opposition speakers that women also initiate and carry out acts of domestic violence, and explained clearly that the bill was intended to benefit women only and to discriminate against men" (Amended complaint 2000, 6). However, the transcript the *Booth* plaintiffs submitted as Exhibit 3 of their complaint indicates that Representative Phyllis Kahn, who introduced the bill, explicitly stated, "We are not saying that every person, every male in this House is a wife beater [any more] than we are saying every male is a rapist" (Amended complaint 2000, exhibit 3).

In the transcript the *Booth* plaintiffs provided, Kahn did not ridicule male victims or deny that they exist. Kahn explained in detail that she had proposed pilot programs tailored to battered women because of women's disproportionate injury, because police failed to enforce assault laws when men assaulted their wives, because battered women had no place to go to escape husbands' violence, and because there existed "a very wide acceptance in society of knocking wives around when they step out of line" (Amended complaint 2000, exhibit 3). Representative Kahn discussed prevalent victim-blaming myths about violence against women—that women stay in relationships because "they're masochistic and encourage the violence"; that "most battered women are frustrated housewives who provoke their husbands into beating them"; and that if women were really being beaten they could simply walk away. Kahn clearly contextualized battered women's disproportionate need for emergency shelter within a cultural context where "police, judges, clergy, doctors, men who beat women, and sadly women who are beaten" endorsed victim-blaming attitudes toward woman abuse. Kahn also made reference to extensive prior testimony before House committees wherein police had apparently testified to the demand and need for services for abused women. Rather than Kahn ridiculing men, the transcript suggests that opponents of the bill were baiting Kahn. Kahn said,

Mr. McDonald speaks very humorously of this issue. This is not a humorous subject. We had fantastic testimony before the committees that this was heard. We had policemen come and tell us of the thousands of women that have been before the St. Paul police, before the police in other cities, who they could do nothing for. The question has been asked at every place that the bill has come up, "Is there a need on an egalitarian basis for this program?" and the answer frankly, Mr. McDonald is no. The [policeman] from St. Paul said he had never in all his years seen a case of a battered man, but in domestic violence and what has been done here and the pictures that he showed were just absolutely shocking. These were not pictures that were dreamed up by a lobbyist, they were pictures taken at Ramsey County Hospital. They were pictures taken at the police station and I don't think you could seriously alter the amendment if you had seen what someone who is exposed to this can end up looking like. If you think there is a problem in the other direction, Mr. McDonald, then you can bring your own bill in or you can offer to double the funding of this bill. (Amended complaint 2000, exhibit 3)

The tactics that representatives opposed to establishing pilot programs for battered women used in the 1970s are very similar to those used today. They changed the subject from documented large numbers of battered women seeking help to anecdotes about abused men and from woman abuse to child abuse. Others objected to talking about the seriousness of men's violence against women because "what you are really saying is that most of us [men] are wife beaters. Are you saying that the majority of males in the State of Minnesota are out beating their wives every day or every night? I just don't think that is right," and "you are saying that women are getting beat and beat and beat by men and men and I don't buy that" (Amended complaint 2000, exhibit 3). The discussion in the Minnesota House of Representatives in 1977 also suggests that representatives opposing the bill were delivering a message about equality with a vengeance. One remarked, "I do submit to the body again, once again, and to Mrs. Kahn that if the precious ERA does become part of the

Constitution of the United States [t]his must read persons," thus suggesting that equal rights for women would mean that addressing women's disproportionate need for emergency shelter was "sexist" (Amended complaint 2000, exhibit 3). Representative Kahn's introduction to the bill made clear that services for battered women in particular were needed because of the ways that ostensibly gender-neutral laws against assault were not being enforced in a gender-neutral way in a cultural context where men's violence against women was condoned, minimized, and blamed on female victims.

 Despite this extensive discussion of battered women's disproportionate need for emergency domestic violence services, the *Booth* plaintiffs asserted that the 1977 bill was intended to discriminate against men. *Booth* argued that even in 1977 research proved that "women initiate and carry out physical assaults on their partners as often as men do, that in some situations women may be more prone to violence than men, and that female violence is, in any event, a major social problem" (Amended complaint 2000, 6).

Following this sex-symmetry claim, the *Booth* plaintiffs produced their fourth exhibit, an annotated bibliography entitled "References Examining Assaults by Women on Their Spouses or Male Partners" (Fiebert 1997) that purportedly documented "the approximately equal rates of domestic violence for men and for women" (Amended complaint 2000, 6). While their discussion of the research evidence was rather incoherent, the *Booth* plaintiffs singled out one chapter cited in the bibliography for discussion as "a well known representative sample from such bibliography" (Amended complaint 2000, 6). That chapter, from the anthology *Current Controversies on Family Violence* (1993), was by Murray Straus and entitled, "Physical Assaults by Wives: A Major Social Problem." The *Booth* plaintiffs quoted Straus's remark that "one can hurt a partner deeply—drive the person to suicide—without ever lifting a finger. Verbal aggression may be even more damaging than physical attacks" (Amended complaint 2000, 7, citing Straus 1993, 67–68). The *Booth* complaint also included lengthy quotes from the chapter itself in which Straus stated that sex differences in rates of physical assaults by husbands and wives were statistically insignificant (Amended complaint 2000, 7, citing Straus 1993, 67–69).

These exhibits reveal the basic structure and content of the *Booth* plaintiffs' argument. The *Booth* plaintiffs claimed that sex differences in domestic violence were insignificant and that women's violence against men was a major social problem. Accordingly, they asserted that domestic violence service providers and printed materials should not acknowledge gender. The *Booth* complaint suggested that services or materials that include battered women's perspectives on violence should be eliminated because they aim to promote discrimination against men, not to address domestic violence. The *Booth* complaint attempted to enforce a way of talking about and responding to woman abuse and other forms of violence against intimates that focused exclusively on individual-level contributing factors to the violence, or perhaps on the interpersonal level where two dysfunctional individuals were presumed to be equally implicated. In rejecting the validity of community- and cultural-level contributing factors to violence, the Booth plaintiffs sought to decontextualize woman abuse decisively.

The Defense Response

The defense team in *Booth v. Hvass* was made up of the defendants, their attorneys, and the defendant-intervenors. Defendant-intervenors are people or organizations that are not initially party to a lawsuit but that align themselves with the defendants as parties to the case because they would likely be affected the decision.

The defense team in *Booth v. Hvass* responded to the lawsuit by addressing multiple aspects of *Booth*'s complaint. The defense challenged the plaintiffs' standing to sue, their characterization of the existing legislation, their representation of the research on violence and abuse, and the allegation that men were denied shelter or other services on the basis of their sex. Each of these elements of the defense response countered the claim of violation of equal protection that was at the core of the case.

In essence, the district court ruled that the plaintiffs did not have standing to sue because they had never been harmed by the statutory scheme they were challenging and because they did not meet the specific and narrow requirements for suing as taxpayers. On appeal, the United States Court of Appeals for the Eighth Circuit upheld that decision. The *Booth* plaintiffs explicitly stated that they had never sought or been denied shelter. Because there was no actual injury to the plaintiffs, the court stated, taxpayer status alone was insufficient legal standing to sue. Although the court never actually addressed the substantive issues around equal protection because the plaintiffs failed to meet the minimum legal requirements for standing, the defense's discussion of these issues is informative and useful beyond the particular case.

On appeal, the defense team argued that the district court's decision was correct in its assessment that the *Booth* plaintiffs lacked standing to sue. In addition, attorneys Beverly Balos and Maury Landsman and student attorneys Karen Olson and Erica Weston argued that the court should ignore the putative evidence of sex symmetry presented by the *Booth* plaintiffs because the research they offered was "subject to dispute, and not capable of easy determination" and thus inadmissible under the rules of evidence (Balos et al. 2001, 8). Furthermore, they observed that upon inspection even the studies the plaintiffs submitted did not support the conclusion that women were as violent as men or that women's violence against men constituted a major social problem.

The *Booth* plaintiffs had simply stapled the annotated bibliography and some articles to their amended complaint rather than following the required legal procedures for submitting expert affidavits (Balos et al. 2001, 7). By contrast, the defense supplemented its argument with an expert affidavit from Dr. Daniel Saunders, then an associate professor at the University of Michigan School of Social Work.[8] Saunders's affidavit reviewed the scientific literature on violence against intimates and disputed the *Booth* plaintiffs' interpretation of it. Saunders also reviewed the documents submitted by the plaintiffs and found that they failed to support claims of sex symmetry. He wrote, "The Plaintiffs' claim that female violence against intimate partners is a major social problem is inaccurate. . . . There is no consensus in the scientific community that violence against men by their intimate partners constitutes a major social problem. However, there is a strong scientific consensus that violence against women by their intimate partners constitutes a major social problem" (Saunders 2001, 3; internal citations omitted).

Saunders noted that the appellants' claim that "women initiate and carry out assaults against their partners as often as men do" is "inaccurate because it is based on speculation or inadequate research" (Saunders 2001, 3; internal citation omitted). He observed that women's and men's violence against intimates is asymmetrical in its outcomes for both lethal and sublethal violence and that the appellants had simply failed to acknowledge studies documenting sex differences, including "police and crime studies that involve the most injurious cases" as well as studies of homicide and separation assault (Saunders 2001, 3). Saunders also pointed out that the studies submitted by the plaintiffs failed to ask about or otherwise account for justifiable forms of violence such as self-defense. As a result, some of the cited articles inappropriately use the term "assault" in discussing their findings although the studies in question cannot discern whether their data indicate assaultive or defensive acts. Saunders also described research documenting the disproportionate effects of men's violence against women in terms of injury and entrapment.

Saunders's affidavit succinctly refuted the existence of a research consensus that women and men are similarly situated with regard to violence by intimates. In reviewing the research submitted and omitted by the plaintiffs in *Booth*, he highlighted the reasons that men's violence against women is qualitatively and quantitatively different than women's violence against men, which undermined the basis of the *Booth* plaintiffs' equal protection claim.[9] His examples illustrated what the authors of Minnesota's statutory scheme funding shelters and other services had argued in 1977—that shelter services for women were an essential part of domestic violence services and that women's need for these services was different from men's.

In answer to the unsubstantiated claim that men were denied domestic violence victim services in Minnesota, the defense submitted affidavits from domestic violence service providers that described the level of demand for services for men and the response to existing requests. For example, Maxine Barnett, executive director of the Central Minnesota Task Force on Battered Women, noted that "during the one year time period of July 1, 1999—June 30, 2000, the task force received only two calls from men inquiring about safe shelter. Both of these calls involved domestic abuse between male partners" (Barnett 2001, 2). In both cases, the task force arranged safe shelter at local hotels, made referrals to additional community services, and assisted the men in securing orders for protection.

Barnett also confirmed that male victims of abuse were already being served in other contexts at the time of the lawsuit, usually in cases where both parties had been charged with a crime. For example, male victims were provided assistance by the Central Minnesota Task Force on Battered Women when they were identified at the hospital as part of a program linking victims of abuse to community resources. The task force also assisted men in preparing orders for protection against male partners and on behalf of child victims. Although no calls were reported from men who sought safe shelter due to abuse by women between July 1, 1999, and June 30, 2000, Barnett noted that "additionally, where appropriate, CMTFBW had advocated for a male victim of domestic abuse to obtain housing" where the man's wife was the abuser (Barnett 2001, 2).

The defense pointed out that men were not in fact denied services because most of the Minnesota legislation was already inclusive of women and men. The only sex-specific source of funding was from the Violence Against Women Act, used to fund freestanding emergency shelters, but these were not the only forms of emergency shelter. Defense attorney Balos observed that the defense affidavits showed that "all of the men who sought shelter services at these programs received shelter services. In fact, the only persons turned away, whose need for shelter was not met for a variety of reasons, were women" (Balos et al. 2001, 6). Thus, contrary to the plaintiffs' claim that men were denied services, these affidavits asserted that men are actually more likely than women to receive the services they request.

Loretta Frederick, attorney for amici curiae, the Minnesota Coalition for Battered Women and the Domestic Violence Legislative Alliance, argued in her brief that the fact that men and women are differently and disproportionately affected by violence is an exceedingly persuasive justification for providing resources targeted at women:

> Based upon years of experience with this issue, the state has focused on providing services to the very victims of domestic violence who they have determined are the most affected by the full range of violence. These victims are the ones most in need of a full range of services, most at risk of future attacks inflicted by their partners, and the most likely to be killed by their abusers. Most, but not all, of these victims are battered women and their children. (Frederick 2001, 9–10)

Frederick cited a Minnesota Supreme Court Task Force report noting that women were victims in 90 percent of more than sixty thousand incidents of domestic violence reported in 1984 (Frederick 2001, 12). In addition to the numeric disparities in domestic violence generally, Frederick pointed out that the risk of lethal domestic violence was also higher for women. She argued, "The lethal nature of domestic violence against women in Minnesota is apparent. . . . The number has grown steadily each year, reaching twenty-two in 1990 and rising to forty in the year 2000" (12). The lethality of the violence and the fact that it often takes place when a woman is trying to leave an abuser make shelters an important resource for battered women.

Responding next to the plaintiffs' criticism of the power and control wheel, Frederick argued that the tool "provides an accurate picture of violence against women" consisting of a "pattern of assaultive and controlling behaviors including physical, sexual, and psychological attacks on the victim, children, property or pets. . . . The pattern goes beyond a single attack and results in a continuing domination over the victim" (2001, 14). According to Frederick, women's violence against men has not followed the same patterns and has tended to be less injurious, less motivated by a desire to control, and more likely to be defensive.

Frederick also pointed out that even the studies relying on decontextualized counts of aggressive acts that *Booth* cited as evidence of sex symmetry found more severe outcomes for women (2001, 15). She also noted research findings indicating that "while men tend to overestimate women's use of violence, women tend to discount or excuse their partners or to blame themselves for men's use of violence against them" (2001, 15–16.) As a result, studies that rely upon estimates of decontextualized aggressive acts seriously distort the realities of violence.

While some sex differences may stem from average physical size differences between women and men, Frederick argued that many of the differences between women's and men's use of violence stem from cultural norms that "have not supported women's use of violence to obtain control over their male partners" (2001, 14). Historically, however, men's violence has been explicitly condoned or simply ignored by the community, with patriarchal social mores shaping women's and men's roles and expectations. Frederick traced the legal, social, and political status of women as subordinate to men and subject to their control and discipline, including violence, and pointed out that the influence of ideas condoning or tolerating abuse of wives by husbands did not die out when all of the states had criminalized domestic violence. Implicit policies of nonintervention meant that police, prosecutors, and counselors often treated violence against wives differently than violence committed by strangers (2001, 19). The same social context that made nonintervention in domestic crimes seem reasonable in the past continued to have impact at the time of *Booth v. Hvass*:

> In the experience of the Amici, battered women frequently report that they are blamed for the violent acts against them, are blamed for not managing to separate safely and early enough from their abusers, and are not supported in their efforts to stop the violence against them. (Frederick 2001, 18–19)

Frederick observed as well that other factors contribute to the difficulties faced by battered women trying to leave an abuser. Isolation— separating women from support systems that might otherwise provide help—is often part of domestic violence. Police and other potential protectors continue to doubt reports of violence. Persistent economic inequality between women and men, exacerbated when women bear the majority of the financial burden of child rearing, further entraps women in abusive relationships.

On the basis of these realities, Frederick asserted that "as the needs of male and female victims of violence in intimate relationships differ substantially, the victim services offered by the state have evolved to reflect their different needs" (2001, 19). Because different treatment of dissimilarly situated individuals is justified under the Fourteenth Amendment, it is justified in the case of domestic violence services. The academic research, crime statistics, and information from service providers provide an exceedingly persuasive justification for providing services tailored to women, who are the majority of adult victims of battering and other forms of systematic domestic abuse. Historical and contemporary gender inequalities compelled Minnesota and other states to respond to a pressing social and public health problem by allocating limited resources where they were most needed. Contrary to the plaintiffs' approach, the defendants sought to position woman abuse decisively within its social ecological context. As the defendants explained, cultural- and community-level factors are essential to understanding why woman abuse happens as well as why specialized resources were established in the first place. Because of the existence of a patriarchal social context, the putatively gender-neutral laws applicable to violence against women were not being enforced in a gender-neutral way when the perpetrators were men and the victims were their female intimate partners.

Because the lawsuit was dismissed, the salient aspects of *Booth v. Hvass* are not the specific details of the legal case but the larger context from which it emerged. The idea of sex symmetry that drove the case was borrowed from other discourses, and symmetry claims continue to be repeated in other contexts. Claims that domestic violence is not a gender issue persist in virtually identical forms and largely cite the same sources. In addition, other lawsuits have attempted to make parallel legal claims with the aim of institutionalizing the idea of domestic violence as sex symmetrical. This social context makes it necessary to scrutinize the core claims at the heart of *Booth v. Hvass*.

3 | Popular Discourses

Booth v. Hvass borrowed its claims and sources from discourses circulating elsewhere in law, media, and scholarship on violence and gender. Issues of terminology, the visibility of perpetrators and victims, and the decontextualization and depoliticization of violence are all relevant to *Booth v. Hvass*. By situating the case within the extant research on popular discourses on woman abuse, the struggle to typify violence against intimates in the *Booth* case and in other locations can be connected. This struggle is both ideological and practical because the outcome has implications for policy responses to violence as well as social norms regarding violence and gender (Bograd 1990a; Dragiewicz 2008). These political implications make woman abuse a frequent subject of commentary among those with both immediate interests in violence policy and more generalized interests in gender politics.

Over the past forty years, woman abuse has dramatically reemerged in the American public consciousness. In the past, wife beating received intermittent publicity, mainly from social reformers and women writers (Pleck 1987). This time around, politicians, lawyers, police officers, and others have joined antiviolence and women's rights advocates in taking up the issue as a national concern. As a result of increasing awareness of violence against women, legislators have enacted a host of legal and policy changes, including VAWA.

In large part because of a few infamous cases involving celebrities and the occasional sensational incident involving ordinary citizens, violence against intimate partners has made a significant impression in popular culture.[1] The mass media's love of the bizarre, the violent, and the famous has helped to ensure that some cases of violence against intimate partners receive a great deal of attention in the United States (McCarthy 1994–95; Thompson 1995). Although more frequent media attention has undoubtedly brought increased awareness of the problem to a broader population, the information media disseminate is often not as good as it could be.

Communication scholars view discourse as a location where competing versions of reality are negotiated. Within that context the research on discourses on woman abuse reveals a struggle between those who believe that gender is a central factor in the etiology of violence and those who believe it is not. The scholarship on violence discourse illustrates the dynamics of hegemony as a dialectical process that incorporates and assimilates challenges to existing power relations. Critical discourse analysis can identify patterns in representations of violence and the effects they engender (Condit 1989; Consalvo 1998b; Meyers 1997).

Scholars who study social problems have used frame analysis, derived from the work of Erving Goffman (1974), to examine how people organize their social experiences and to identify competing "frames," or ways of understanding complex social problems (Berns 2004). The dominant frames for woman abuse can be characterized as feminist or antifeminist. Following Nancy Berns, I define antifeminist discourses as those that are more focused on attacking feminism than addressing woman abuse (Berns 2001, 2004). Antifeminist frames are used to describe violence against intimates while undermining feminism and its affiliated categories—gender and patriarchy. These frames seek to contain the threat that recognizing men's violence against women poses to the existing social order (Berns 2004; Lamb 1991; McKay and Smith 1995; Meyers 1997; Steeves 1997). Feminist frames highlight the cultural, social, and structural contexts of woman abuse in order to help prevent it. The presence of both feminist and antifeminist frames in popular discourses highlights the struggle to promote very different understandings of woman abuse (Berns 2004; Stone 1993).

Wini Breines and Linda Gordon commented on this struggle as early as 1983, when the first wave of "sex-neutral" approaches to violence research threatened to circumvent consideration of patriarchy, power, gender, and control in discussions of woman abuse. Breines and Gordon argued that discourses on violence that omit gender as a category of analysis are motivated by a desire to explain away realities that are too uncomfortable for nonfeminists to confront. They also point out that such discourses not only obscure the true nature of violence but discourage productive analysis of it (Breines and Gordon 1983).

Contemporary discourse on woman abuse emerged from feminist political discussions of the problem during the late 1960s and early 1970s

(Schechter 1982), but it has lost much of its feminist political orientation in the process of assimilation into mainstream media and scholarly contexts (Berns 2001, 2004; Lerman 1992). For example, Ann Jones has noted the pervasive use of the "language of love" in media accounts of violence against women. She has argued, "This slipshod reporting has real consequences in the lives of real men and women. It affirms the batterer's most common excuse for assault: 'I did it because I love you'" (Jones 1994, A4). The research on attributions of responsibility for violence supports Jones's observation. Violence understood as caused by excessive passion is perceived as less deviant and more acceptable than other violence, at least when perpetrated by men (Cerulo 1998).

Research on discourses on woman abuse has identified several primary patterns—increased visibility of woman abuse, the decontextualization and depoliticization of this type of violence, and the reaffirmation of existing social hierarchies. However, the visibility of woman abuse has not consistently increased over time. Media and scholarly interest in the issue ebbed and flowed prior to the latest feminist articulation of wife battering in the 1960s and 1970s (Breines and Gordon 1983; Gordon 1988; Schneider 2000). The decontextualization and depoliticization of violence are serious impediments to decreasing its occurrence; by obscuring the very conditions that produce violence, decontextualized discourses on violence can preserve those conditions. The need to address the problem on a broad cultural scale is also minimized when discourses on woman abuse explain it as a product of communities already marginalized according to immigrant, racial minority, or low socioeconomic status (Kozol 1995; Meyers 1997). Such discourses serve to affirm the legitimacy of existing social hierarchies based on class, immigration status, and race.

Antifeminist Discourses on Woman Abuse

In the United States, the public debate over whether woman abuse is a gendered phenomenon is perhaps most intense on antifeminist websites, which alternately identify themselves as antifeminist, men's rights, men's issues, or fathers' rights sites (Dragiewicz 2008; Menzies 2007; Rosen, Dragiewicz, and Gibbs 2009). Magazines from *New Republic* to *Mother Jones* and *Reason* and more mainstream publications including *U.S. News and World Report* also feature articles attacking approaches to woman abuse that acknowledge its gendered character. Such high-circulation newspapers as the *New York Times* and the *Washington Post* and, to a lesser degree, smaller-circulation community newspapers also cover the debate. In newspapers the debate rages most frequently in the opinion and letters pages. Berns found that pornographic magazines including *Penthouse* and *Playboy* use antifeminist frames similar to those found in such political media as *National Review,* which highlights the overlap between representations in political and entertainment media (2004). In the mass media, claims that intimate violence is not gendered often take an explicitly antifeminist approach. One August 1994 article in *National Review* stated,

> It did not take long for advocacy groups and some commentators to claim that the O. J. Simpson case could do for domestic violence what Anita Hill did for sexual harassment. If the Anita Hill analogy refers to gender politics eclipsing truth, common sense, and journalistic skepticism, then that is exactly what's happening." (Young 1994, 43)

The following year another *National Review* article argued that efforts to stop woman abuse cast men in an unfair light. "In the current climate of hysteria, those who question conventional wisdom are denounced as enemies of women," the writer noted. "Radical feminists are using the issues of domestic violence and rape to create a new jurisprudence that assesses guilt and imposes punishment based on gender" (McElroy 1995, 74). A 1995 *New Republic* article declared, "Radical women's groups actively oppose the spreading of more accurate information about gender equity in family violence" (Dunn 1994, 18). In the same year an article in *U.S. News and World Report* alleged similarly. "These days, it's fairly routine to see journalism endorsing the radical theory of domestic violence as gender warfare. Domestic violence can be portrayed as a war against women, but only if a lot of evidence is suppressed or explained away" (Leo 1994, 22).

Efforts to undermine feminism are often explicit in such commentaries, which characterize woman abuse as gender-free. Rather than contributing to a solution for violence, these articles focus on discrediting abused women, advocates, and scholars who seek to contextualize violence in order to prevent it. These tactics are mirrored in the *Booth* complaint.

Jennifer Pozner has observed that research on violence against intimates is often labeled ideology or science based not upon its methodology or the qualifications of the person conducting the research but upon the outcome of the study. She noted that U.S. Department of Justice research has been labelled both, based on the findings of the particular study (1999):

Researchers whose findings show that domestic violence is predominately perpetrated by men to exercise control over their female partners are often [portrayed as] "feminist theorists" orchestrating a "myth-making industry" to promote "half-truths based on ideological dogma," as columnist Kathleen Parker wrote. Conversely, the handful of researchers whose studies find that battery is committed equally by men and women may be labeled as scientific "pioneers" pursuing hard facts and empirically sound data. (Pozner 1999; internal citations omitted)

Booth echoed the tendency to characterize as ideology rather than as scholarship all research that acknowledges gender and patriarchy as contributing factors to violence.

Ironically, gender shows up especially vividly in one particular version of the antifeminist claim that violence against intimates is not gendered. Antifeminist writers frequently assert that so few police and medical reports of women battering men exist because men report being victimized by intimate partners much less often than women do. While antifeminists use this claim to promote degendered understandings of violence, they explain this alleged difference in reporting in ways explicitly tied to patriarchal gender norms for hegemonic masculinity:

Men who are abused by their wives are fodder for jokes. Women who are abused by their husbands can get away with murder (Dunn 1994, 17).

The one defining characteristic of most abused men is that they are extremely embarrassed by their predicament. Most men who have reached out for help have been laughed at or scorned. They are often portrayed as weak and cowardly (Menweb 2010).

Men are also less likely to call the police, even when there is injury, because, like women, they feel shame about disclosing family violence. But for many men, the shame is compounded by the shame of not being able to keep their wives under control. Among this group, a 'real man' would be able to keep her under control. Moreover, the police tend to share these same traditional gender role expectations (Free Republic 2005).

In 18th- and 19th-century France, a husband who had been pushed around by his wife would be forced by the community to wear women's clothing and to ride through the village, sitting backwards on a donkey, holding its tail. . . . This humiliating practice, called the charivari, was also common in other parts of Europe. . . . Modern versions of the charivari persist today. Take Skip W., who participated in a program on domestic violence aired on the short-lived Jesse Jackson Show in 1991. Skip related how his wife repeatedly hit him and attacked him with knives and scissors. The audience's reaction was exactly what male victims who go public fear most: laughter, and constant, derisive snickering (Brott 1994).

These writers implicate the rigid, polarized gender norms enforced in patriarchal societies as the primary reason that violence against men is not taken seriously. Above all they point to the threat of feminization, made menacing by the low status accorded to the feminine in patriarchal societies, as a shaming tactic used to punish men who fail to dominate their wives or partners. This kind of enforcement of hegemonic masculinity is precisely what feminists mean to indicate when they discuss violence as a gendered phenomenon. In addition, these quotations hint at the disparate risks faced by female and male survivors of abuse. The meaning and outcomes of violence vary according to the relative status and resources of both partners, and there is still much to learn about these variations and their impact on the dynamics of abuse and reporting or seeking services. However, it is clear even from these antifeminist explanations for the low numbers of men reporting violence that patriarchal gender norms are to blame and are potentially harmful to men as well as to women.

Such high-profile incidents as the O. J. Simpson case have contributed disproportionately to the visibility of woman abuse in the media (Stone 1993). Sheryl McCarthy (1994–95) has noted that news coverage of these cases generated increased attention to violence and commonly blamed the victim, identified the batterer as the "real" victim, and misrepresented feminism. As a result, powerful evidence such as photographs of a bruised Nicole Brown Simpson and recordings of her 911 calls helped educate the public about the horrors of woman abuse even as stereotypes about women as selfish gold-diggers served to mitigate the perpetrator's responsibility for violence. McCarthy's research illustrates how media coverage of woman abuse, even of the same case, conveys contradictory messages with similarly contradictory outcomes for public understandings of violence.

The decontextualization of violence against women is also visible in approaches that identify it as pathological, rare, unpredictable, or solely a criminal justice problem. Wendy Kozol's research (1995) highlights the ways in which media discourse focuses on individual free will and deviance instead of the hierarchical social relations that promote violence.

Kozol argued that media coverage of violence against women serves to reinforce the American language of individual "choice" and ignores the material and social constraints of race, class, and gender hierarchies that shape personal choices.

For example, Kozol observed that in the film *Sleeping with the Enemy,* the abused woman character Laura Burney's efforts to escape from her abuser are located exclusively in the private sphere. Rather than reaching out to the public-sphere resources that exist to help battered women, Laura Burney escapes from her affluent husband by running alone to a small town where her new boyfriend is the only one who helps her (1995, 654). By ignoring all of the resources that exist to assist abused women, *Sleeping with the Enemy* and similarly individualizing depictions of women leaving their abusers circumvent questions about the ways in which women are disproportionately likely to become entrapped in abusive heterosexual relationships. Individualized representations of abused women's escape from abusers also skirt the issue of the adequacy and effectiveness of public-sphere responses to violence.

Neil Websdale and Alexander Alvarez observed that media coverage of violence against women rarely goes beyond what they have termed "forensic journalism" (1997). Reporting normally focuses on the specific details of a case, they have argued, without noting whether or how it fits into the larger dynamics of violence as a patterned social problem. This decontextualization creates a missed opportunity for prevention and education (Websdale and Chesney-Lind 1998). Celeste Condit (1989) suggested that this kind of decontextualization makes it difficult for readers to gain accurate understandings of the dynamics of violence and abuse. Many of the scholars who have studied media discourses on violence against women have emphasized this trend toward decontextualization (Davis 2000; Ferraro 1996; Hearn 1998; Klein 1997; Lerman 1992; McKay and Smith 1995; Meyers 1997). Breines and Gordon remarked on the importance of contextualizing violence in their 1983 review of the emerging research on violence in the family. "Once discrete acts of violence, removed from overall power relations, become the subject of the study, the 'data' no longer describe reality," they argued (1983, 513).

The alternative to viewing violence against intimates in its social context is to regard it as an individual problem. Crime and deviance discourses focus on the maintenance of the current social order, rather than its alteration, by focusing on individual transgression rather than the larger social and institutional patterns that may promote crime and violence (Davis 2000; Ferraro 1996; Klein 1997; Meyers 1997; Phillips and Henderson 1999). Kathleen Ferraro (1996) has discussed how framing violence against women as a crime problem can promote legal responses to the most blatant forms of abuse. However, legal responses cannot prevent violence; only changes in the cultural environment that engenders violence can decrease its incidence. Legal changes alone cannot bring about such social progress. Ferraro argues that individualizing conceptualizations of violence against women diminish the possibility that the hegemonic view will perceive violence as a social problem with social causes and solutions. As a result, she has argued, the public both condemns violence and opposes the very changes that might prevent it.

Contrary to feminist discourses on woman abuse that highlight social inequality, the highly visible crime control discourse draws from existing stereotypes in order to reinforce the social order that helps produce violence in the first place (Berns 2001, 2004; Ferraro 1996; Meyers 1997; Schneider 2000). Although the increased visibility of violence against women as a crime has benefited many women by providing them with increased access to emergency services and shelter, current discourses fail to serve many other women living with violence. As Angela Davis has argued, repoliticizing the discourse is essential to preventing domestic violence and intervening on behalf of those women and men the anti-violence discourse does not serve well, including both women of color who are victims of male violence and the men of color who are disproportionately targeted by the criminal justice system (Davis 2000).

In addition to media representations of violence focused on crime control, representations of woman abuse as pathological are also common (Meyers 1997). Pathologizing violence means treating it as a literal or figurative form of disease. Talking about violence as a problem of "sick" individuals often erases the social forces that contribute to the violence, from economic to cultural factors (Klein 1997; McKay and Smith 1995; Meyers 1997; Websdale and Chesney-Lind 1998). Because descriptions of violence as pathological often treat it as the product of an innate or irreversible defect, they also render prevention efforts unlikely and inappropriate (Meyers 1997). The plaintiffs in *Booth v. Hvass* invoked pathologizing discourses on violence when they equated it with alcoholism and advised treatment rather than criminal penalties or broad-based social change to deal with it.

As Ferraro (1996) observed, decontextualizing violence also depoliticizes it by obscuring the relationship between institutionalized and informal power relations and violence. Many scholars who study violence argue that because woman abuse is a pattern of ongoing, coercive, and controlling behavior, decontextualizing it creates a particularly distorted view of the problem and its potential solutions (Berns 2001; Dasgupta 2002; DeKeseredy 2000; Dobash and Dobash 1998; Lerman 1992; Stark 2007). *Booth v. Hvass* expressed a similar decontextualization in its emphasis on individual victims of abuse rather than on the context in which abuse takes place. By focusing only on the number of individuals being served, the *Booth* plaintiffs argued that women's disproportionate use of services was a sign of advantage over men. According to this framing, women's greater demand for domestic violence-related services was actually a sign of female privilege. The *Booth* plaintiffs argued that eliminating state support for the services women use more than men would eliminate this inequity. Yet framing violence in this way ignores women's disproportionate victimization by male partners. Eliminating services would increase women's vulnerability to violence and exacerbate the very circumstances that cause women's disproportionate demand for service.

Depoliticizing violence also obscures power relations in other ways. Discourses on violence against women have historically directed attention toward certain already marginalized social groups. The research on violence discourse finds, in accordance with established stereotypes about men, violence, and masculinities, widespread patterns of invisibility for white, middle- and upper-class male perpetrators and greater visibility for men who are racial or ethnic minorities, poor, alcoholic, mentally ill, or immigrant (Dasgupta 2002; Davis 2000; Dobash and Dobash 1979; Ferraro 1996; Gordon 1988; McCarthy 1994–95; Meyers 1997; Pleck 1987). These discourses help to justify and maintain current hierarchies of power. For example, Mia Consalvo's analysis of the television show *Cops* found recurring messages about class and alcohol use that created an unchallenged association of poverty and drunkenness with violence against women (1998b). Crime-control discourses make it easy for journalists and others to describe abuse as perpetrated by the same marginalized groups of men already targeted by criminal justice policy and practice. Such discourses ensure that white, middle- and upper-class, heterosexual men remain largely absent from discourses on violence. The invisibility of the intersections of race, class, gender, and sexuality that bell hooks

(1984) has termed "white-supremacist-capitalist-patriarchy" is maintained when privileged white men are left out of the conversation about crime problems.

While marginalized men are disproportionately visible in discourses on violence against women, patriarchal privilege also shapes representations of violence. Masculinity or maleness rarely factor into antifeminist discussions about violence (Hearn 1998; Johnson 2005). Researchers, journalists, and service providers often ignore or imply the sex of the male perpetrator in woman abuse cases. In a study of scholarly representations of men who batter, Sharon Lamb (1991) found multiple forms of "linguistic avoidance" that served to obscure men's disproportionate perpetration of violence, including use of the passive voice to describe men's violence, nominalization of the violence (changing it from an act to a thing), and the use of diffuse terminology to describe violence. Lamb has argued that writing about violence must clearly indicate the identities of perpetrators and victims.

Debby Phillips and Dorothy Henderson found similar patterns in their review of scholarly and popular writing on domestic violence (1999). Phillips and Henderson argued that the invisibility of men in violence discourse frames woman abuse as a problem for women instead of a problem with male behavior. Further, obfuscating male violence creates ambiguous texts that can be perceived as discussing violent women when they are in fact describing men's violence against women. In such cases, degendered language may promote inaccurate understandings of the dynamics of violence. Phillips and Henderson suggested that this kind of unclear discourse on violence has contributed to the idea that women are as violent as men and that violence against intimates is "mutual combat," despite research evidence to the contrary.

Geraldine Finn (1989) documented a similar lack of discussion of men as perpetrators of violence in news coverage of woman abuse, international terrorism, and the effects of violence in the media. Finn observed that the invisibility of men as objects for analysis in discourses on violence serves to maintain the centrality of their experiences.

> The gender-specificity of violence, of the discourses of violence, and of the effects/affects of its representation in the media, is not acknowledged in debates about media [representations of] violence, all of which thereby assume the standpoint of men, as if there were no other, as if it were gender-neutral. (388)

All of these forms of erasure serve to keep men as a group relatively invisible in discourses on violence and to ensure that men's experiences remain the taken-for-granted norm.

In contrast, women are highly visible in discourses on woman abuse. This visibility has garnered public support for some victims of violence, but, as is the case with representations of men, it matters what kind of woman one is. Women who fit normative ideals for femininity and behavior may be treated sympathetically, but those who do not are often blamed for the violence done to them (Berns 2004; Breines and Gordon 1983). Consalvo's study of news coverage of the murder of a mail-order bride and two of her friends at the courthouse as she was attempting to divorce her abuser illustrates this pattern. In this case, Consalvo found that mainstream coverage of the killings pathologized the male perpetrator, obscured the history of violence that preceded the murder, and validated the killer's characterization of the woman he murdered as blameworthy (1998a).

In her study *News Coverage of Violence Against Women* (1997), Marian Meyers found that research findings on media representations of "crime" in general did not apply to coverage of violent crimes against women. The media scholars whom Meyers termed "crime-as-deviance theorists" have claimed that criminals "are presented as deviants whose actions are outside the limits of acceptable social behavior and who, therefore, deserve to be shunned by all law-abiding citizens" (23). However, this "generalization," based on attention to representations of men, does not accurately describe news treatment of violent crimes against women, which generally serves as a warning to women to behave themselves according to patriarchal gender norms and tends to emphasize the victim's behavior rather than the perpetrator's. Such media accounts pay less attention to the specifics of the crime than to the social acceptability of the victim's actions, dress, or lifestyle (Meyers 1997). Newspaper coverage often denies sympathy to women who fight back against abusers because it casts women's violence as unnatural or monstrous (Breines and Gordon 1983; Cerulo 1998; Gilbert 2002; Leonard 2002; Schneider 2000). The scholars Meyers has cited fail to mention that their studies of media discourses involve only men's crimes against men, a point that again illustrates the invisible, taken-for-granted centrality of men's experiences.

Virtually every study on the discourses on woman abuse cite victim blaming and casting doubt on the woman's virtue as perhaps the most common aspects of news coverage of the subject. Victim blaming is less blatant in scholarly discourses on woman abuse, but research continues to focus on female victims' behavior and attributes, especially in research that regards such violence as gender-neutral or mutual combat.[2]

Overall, the research on discourses on woman abuse documents its increasing visibility over the past four decades, which has contributed to increased funding and attention for antiviolence work and increased availability of services. However, the visibility of woman abuse as a social problem has not supplanted the ideas that victims precipitate violence or that already marginalized men perpetrate it. Instead, feminist framings of violence as a social problem with political solutions coexist alongside more conservative understandings of violence. The juxtaposition of competing frames reveals the ongoing struggle to typify violence.

The plaintiffs in *Booth v. Hvass* drew upon many of these common ways of talking about violence. They relied upon decontextualized and depoliticized discourses about violence to shore up their claim that women's disproportionate demand for services constitutes discrimination against men rather than disparate need. They based this claim on a myopic focus on individual-level contributing factors to violence to the exclusion of community and cultural contributing factors. The *Booth* complaint also drew heavily on specific representations of violence as sex-symmetrical and gender-blind notions that also contain contradictory messages about the nature of violence. The meaning of these contradictions does not become fully clear, however, until they are juxtaposed with the ways that batterers talk about their violence.

Alcoholic wife — Easy to blame

4 | Batterer Narratives

When examined outside their historical and political contexts, competing discourses on violence and abuse might appear to be equally valid. Reasonable people can disagree about how to measure and understand violence and abuse and what terms to use when writing about them. However, the choice to highlight or obscure particular dynamics of violence and the context in which it occurs has implications for knowledge, safety, and social justice.

The research on men who abuse women has frequently found that men use violence to produce and defend patriarchal masculinities (Bowker 1998; DeKeseredy and Schwartz 1998; Messerschmidt 1993, 1999, 2000, 2004; Moore and Stuart 2005; Smith 1990, 1991; Totten 2003). Hegemonic masculinity is not only a factor in men's violence against women; it is also an important feature of men's violence against other men (Gilligan 1997, 2001; Messerschmidt 1993, 1997, 1999, 2000, 2004). The scholarship on masculinities has stressed that the social norms for masculinity include multiple masculinities that are relevant in different social and historical contexts (Connell 2000, 2002; Connell and Messerschmidt 2005).

Because the greatest risk to men of violent victimization, including physical and sexual assault, comes from other men, addressing the links between masculinity and violence is an essential part of decreasing men's use of and risk from violence across the board. The rich empirical research on men's accounts of their violence is an underutilized resource for understanding violence as a social problem. While some factors contributing to violence—such as poverty, mental illness, or addiction—may be similar for women and men, these factors cannot explain men's disproportionate use of violence relative to women. Because research indicates that patriarchal gender norms play a role in the etiology of men's violence against women and men, gender is an important factor that can help explain why men are more likely to use violence than women, and why some groups of men are more likely to use violence than others.

Much as Diana Scully and Joseph Marolla (1985) documented the function of rape for convicted rapists, this chapter investigates the function of violence for male batterers. The accounts of men who batter women comprise one of the most salient sources for understanding *Booth v. Hvass*. Batterer accounts are also relevant to other attacks on gender-inclusive responses to violence that seek to eliminate services targeting battered women. The research on factors contributing to men's violence against women may not be relevant to women's violence against men due to the significant quantitative and qualitative differences in women's and men's use of violence. Research comparing why and how women and men use force in relationships has consistently found sex-disparate patterns and has indicated divergent etiologies for women's and men's violence (Anderson and Umberson 2001; Dasgupta 2002; Edleson and Brygger 1986; Hamberger and Guse 2002; Osthoff 2002).

Although there are now literally thousands of books and articles on violence against intimates, only a small body of work focuses directly on male batterers' perspectives on their violence. One reason for the relative dearth of studies on male batterers is the difficulty of gaining access to men who are willing to participate in research. Still, an accessible pool of potential respondents has been identified among incarcerated batterers, batterers participating in programs, and survey participants who report using violence.

Though it makes sense to pay attention to what batterers say about why they use violence and what they get out of it in order to understand it better, batterers' accounts of what happened should not necessarily be taken at face value. What batterers say about violence can help us understand why they use violence as well as how they justify and continue that violence in the face of nominal cultural disapproval. Attention to batterer narratives reveals points of overlap between what is ostensibly deviant behavior and the hegemonic norms sustaining it. James Ptacek observed in his study of batterers that "not only do they present their violence in a light that illuminates its intentionality and cruelty, but their words also reveal the blind spots in the dominant clinical perspectives" (Ptacek 1990, 133). Identifying these points makes it possible to recognize them in other locations and to begin to address their implications.

The frames batterers use to talk about violence are remarkably similar to those underlying *Booth v. Hvass*. The tactics of denial, minimization, justification, and excuse are central to both batterer narratives and the *Booth* case. Batterer accounts of violence also support feminist and other research on the importance of patriarchy to violence. According to violent men's accounts, patriarchal gender norms are frequently a key factor in their use of violence against women. Because patriarchal masculinities play such a central role in men's batterer narratives, leaving gender out seriously impedes efforts to understand such violence.

Feminist efforts to increase awareness of woman abuse and research on the problem have contributed to a decrease in blatant victim blaming. Early publications on wife-beating posited that batterers were "shy, sexually ineffectual, reasonably hard working 'mother's boys with a tendency to drink excessively'" while the women they beat were "aggressive, efficient, masculine and sexually frigid" (Snell et al. 1964, 111). These early articles showed more concern about understanding why women called police on their abusers than about changing the violent behavior, because the "husband's behavior may serve to fill a wife's need even though she protests it" (Snell et al. 1964, 110). The belief in female masochism as a key cause of battering persisted in scholarship into the 1980s (Hilberman 1980). Then as now, scholars who critiqued victim blaming were chastised for having a "feminist axe to grind" and accused of political rather than scholarly motives. In a response to Elaine Hilberman's critique of theories positing female masochism as the primary cause of wife beating, Glen Gabbard and Jan Larson argued,

> Masochism is not a myth. It is prevalent in individuals who remain in situations that lead to repeated suffering. Theories of masochism do not claim that the wife-beater's wife is at fault for her husband's physical attacks. They propose that there is an unconscious collusion between the persecutor (sadist) and the victim (masochist). We agree with Dr. Hilberman that sadomasochistic relationships operating on an unconscious level do not entirely explain the phenomenon. However, an understanding of these unconscious forces operating in such dyads is an important part of the picture. (1981, 533)

Gabbard and Larson's view is not as archaic as it might seem. One of the primary arguments in *Booth* was that "abusing women (and those who unconsciously solicit abuse) are not given the chance to be accountable for their own actions" (R-KIDS 2001, 6). One reason to pay more attention to batterer narratives is that public discourses on violence continue to focus overwhelmingly on women. The *Booth* plaintiffs objected to abused women being seen as credible witnesses and being offered services tailored to their disproportionate needs due to men's violence against them. However, popular attention to violence and abuse hardly resembles the total credulity of police and judges alleged in the case. "Why didn't she just leave?" continues to be an exceedingly common question asked about battered women.

Contrary to *Booth's* complaint and other antifeminist discourses, attention to men's violence against women has always been met with resistance. Scholars have stood on both sides of this political debate from the start. Since the earliest efforts to have violence against women taken seriously, antifeminist scholars and commentators have sought to create the appearance of battering as a problem equally shared and caused by both women and men, to deflect attention from men's violence against women as an undeniably visible social problem to the contention that an army of "battered men" exists (Dobash and Dobash 1979; Steinmetz 1977–78).

At the same time that they see any report of violence against men as proof of women's equal violence, many antifeminist commentators insist that feminists have inflated estimates of men's violence against women (Brott 1994; Dunn 1994; Leo 1994; Young 1994). Claims of parity in violence against intimates have consistently been used in campaigns to discredit feminism and have largely relied on the same measurement tool, the Conflict Tactics Scales (CTS),[1] and on the same arguments invoked since the 1970s.

Because antifeminist frames distort violence by focusing attention on decontextualized counts of a small set of acts, the realities of violence to which these numbers refer must be acknowledged. While statistical estimates on the prevalence of violence are complicated and difficult for most people to understand, batterer narratives provide concrete examples of the dynamics of violence that cause battered women to call the police or to seek shelter in order to escape. Quantitative measures of violence and its contributing factors are important, but batterers' qualitative accounts of why they use violence are also a very useful source of information.

A small but remarkably consistent literature documents heterosexual male batterers' descriptions of their violence, including their perceptions of their violent actions, how they imagine the outcomes of their violence, and their motives for battering female partners. This wealth of information about why heterosexual male abusers do what they do has thus far been inadequately applied to efforts to understand and decrease woman abuse. By looking at men's accounts of battering, we can begin to understand the social forces that contribute to violence, the frames that batterers use in descriptions of their violence, and the way these two factors intersect to allow abusers to justify, excuse, deny, and minimize their violence. Studying how batterers account for their violence also reveals connections to other discourses.

The research on batterer narratives is drawn mostly from batterers who have been involved with the criminal justice system, treatment programs, or both—what is sometimes called a "clinical sample" rather than a "representative sample" (Straus 1990a). Thus, these narratives reflect manifestations of violence that are serious enough to push victims or others to seek outside intervention in the abuse. Although these cases may not be representative of all aggression or conflict between family members, by definition they reflect the kinds of violence that battered women's shelters, orders for protection, and other interventions were created to ameliorate. As such, batterer narratives are potentially a more relevant source of information about the kinds of violence relevant to battered women's shelters and other service providers than numbers gleaned from quantitative surveys using statistically representative samples.

If men's violence against women were universally condemned, as antifeminist discourses often claim it to be, we could expect batterers simply to deny being violent. However, batterer narratives contain a more complicated combination of rhetorical tactics. Many abusers frankly discuss their reasons for using violence, and many concede a wide array of violent and abusive behaviors.

Glen Stamp and Teresa Chandler Sabourin (1995) drew from social science research on the function of accounts of personal experiences to understand batterer narratives. They argued that because accounts are stories of events about which a value judgment may be made, they can provide useful information about batterers' perspectives by revealing how they negotiate what are often conflicting social norms, personal beliefs, and interpersonal behaviors. Internal contradictions in batterer narratives point to the abusers' awareness of contradictory social messages. On the one hand men are enjoined to "never hit a girl." On the other hand batterers employ a rich vocabulary of justifications and explanations for violence in efforts to avoid censure for their violent actions (Dutton 1986; Ptacek 1990; Stamp and Sabourin 1995).

The research consistently identifies abusers' use of four major tactics to account for their violence—denial, minimization, justification, and excuse. Abusers tend to use multiple rhetorical strategies, even during a single account (Hearn 1998). These contradictions mirror the mixed messages about men's violence toward women identified by research conducted in other contexts (McCarry 2009; Weiss 2009). The grouping of abuser comments into these categories is somewhat arbitrary in view of the fact that many statements could fit in multiple categories. For example, a man who kills his wife's dog might explain his actions as "self-defense" because his wife hurt his feelings first, and he might also minimize his violence by adding that while he killed the dog he never touched *her*; thus he is not really abusive. However, grouping the different tactics into categories makes it easier to focus on the function of the tactic rather than being diverted into debates about the legitimacy of a litany of individual claims. Identifying particular rhetorical tactics makes it easier to recognize the connections between cases and thus to reveal the structural factors that contribute to the prevalence of violence. Bancroft (2002) has argued that batterers themselves have created much of the widely accepted mythology about abusive men through careful manipulation of public appearances. Identifying the overlap between batterers' accounts of their violence and other accounts has the potential to highlight the implications of accounts that mimic those of batterers. Batterer accounts of violence also irrefutably identify the gendered dimensions of violence that antifeminists consistently disavow.

Denial

Victor Robinson (1994) has identified five kinds of personal and cultural denial that surround child abuse and woman abuse and that abusers, victims, their family and friends, the community, researchers, and the culture in general often share—denial that the act happened, denial that what happened was criminal, denial that what happened caused significant harm, denial of intention or control, and denial of responsibility (Robinson 1994). Although other scholars have categorized some of these kinds of denial as minimization or justification, Robinson's typology illustrates how different ways of accounting for violence can have common implications. Thus, denial that abuse caused harm also minimizes the significant effects of violence.

Batterers' accounts indicate categories of denial in addition to those Robinson has identified—denial that the abuser perpetrated the violence, denial that the abuser is a violent or abusive person, and denial that the abuser knows what happened. Denial is illustrated by numerous batterers' comments:

> I only threatened her (Pence and Paymar 1993, 77).
>
> Hit her? I did everything *but* hit her (Stamp and Sabourin 1995, 296).
>
> No, I'm not a violent person. I have to be really, really provoked. I'm just so placid. It takes me a long time to wind up, a long time. Somebody has to really hurt me before I'm wound up. Anybody will tell you, I'm not a violent person. I'm not violent. I've never been in court for violence or anything. . . . I can look after myself, don't get me wrong, but I try to avoid it (Hearn 1998, 110).
>
> I was charged on murder, an attempt, which they say I could have done it, but coulds and ifs are no good, unless they are positive, and I have been pleading my innocence since they brought me [to the prison] (Hearn 1998, 110).
>
> I wouldn't say I was violent. Violence is not a part of me (Cavanagh et al. 2001, 701).[2]
>
> There was no violence towards [partner] though she would have you believe there was (Cavanagh et al. 2001, 701).
>
> I was never violent, just bad tempered (Cavanagh et al. 2001, 701).
>
> I never beat my wife. I responded physically to her (Ptacek 1990, 146).

Denial that the abuser perpetrated the violence is fairly straightforward. It may include denial that anything violent happened or more elaborate stories about how the victim came to hurt herself through no fault of the abuser. Batterers often deny that they are violent people or at least that they would ever hit a woman. In this way, batterers apparently seek to create the impression that nice guys like them simply could not have perpetrated violence. This form of denial feeds on stereotypes about batterers as instantly recognizable cruel monsters. Batterers often cultivate positive public images in order to conceal their violence and maintain their self-image as great guys (Bancroft 2002). Batterers' insistence that they are nice or not violent people is mirrored in public accounts of domestic homicide; interviews with neighbors who invariably testify about what a nice guy the abuser was are a staple of news coverage. In the *Booth* case, denial appears as the claim that women's reports of violence are false. In this case, reports of violence to the police or that cause women to seek shelter are denied in favor of an explanation that women are liars who make false allegations against innocent men at the urging of feminists.

In other cases, denial takes the form of "forgetting" or "not knowing" what happened. For example, abusers make such statements as, "I can't really go into detail because I just can't remember it all" (Hearn 1998, 113). Abusers often admit to some bad behavior and simultaneously claim to "forget" other aspects of their violence.

> I can remember the ripping her clothes off, but not the raping bit. . . . I can't remember (Hearn 1998, 149).

> I remember it all happened that fast. I remember hitting her but I couldn't tell you where, and I can remember flinging the glass but apart from that I can't remember hitting her (Cavanagh et al. 2001, 702).

Jeff Hearn (1998) observed that denial often occurs in the same narrative alongside detailed accounts of (or for) the violence. For example, even batterers who admitted to many violent acts often denied that they could recall or describe specific events when asked about them. Michele Bograd (1988) noted that while one might expect batterers' accounts to be internally consistent, they often are not. For example, even when batterers disavow violence, they are often careful to emphasize their strength, size, and capacity to use violence if they want to. These juxtapositions suggest that despite the men's denial of certain forms of transgressive violence, their perceptions of normative masculinity call for the capacity to do violence.

In addition to the qualitative research on denial in batterer narratives, quantitative research suggests that men often deny their abuse of women and that they are more likely to deny certain kinds of violence that are widely regarded as unacceptable. Men have been found to underreport violence that would be seen as unambiguously abusive, such as punching a pregnant woman in the stomach, as well as forms of violence that might be considered gender-inappropriate for men, such as scratching and biting (Arias and Beach 1987; Dobash, Dobash, Cavanagh, and Lewis 1998; Szinovacz 1983).

Minimization

Closely related to denial is minimization of the nature, frequency, and number of violent incidents and their outcomes. The research documenting men's and women's disparate accounts of violence suggests that male abusers may minimize their violence by categorizing it as something less than violent. Male batterers underreport both the frequency and seriousness of their own violence (Arias and Beach 1987; Bancroft 2002; Dobash et al. 1992; Dobash et al. 1998; Szinovacz 1983). Some batterers minimize their violence by making favorable comparisons between their behavior and other men's behavior or by drawing a distinction between their own behavior and what they consider to be violence or abuse:

> These people told her that she had to get all these orders of protection and stuff like that because I'm going to kill her, you know. Well I wasn't going to kill her. I mean I'd yell at her, and scream and stuff like that, and maybe I'd whack her once or twice, you know, but I wasn't going to kill her. That's for sure (Ptacek 1990, 146).
>
> I wasn't violent but she used to do my head in that much. I picked her up twice and threw her against the wall, and said "just leave it." That's the only violence I've put towards her. I've never struck a woman, never, and I never will. . . . When I held her I did bruise her somewhere on the shoulder, and she tried making out that I'd punched her, but I never did. I never to this day touched a woman (Hearn 1998, 117).
>
> I'm not really into violence. I've only ever been violent to Fiona. I've never been violent to anybody else (Cavanagh et al. 2001, 702).
>
> I know I hit her but I definitely didn't batter her (Cavanagh et al. 2001, 706).

Abusers often minimize acts of violence that women have specifically reported:

> It wasn't really abuse. . . . Before I married my woman she was married to an abuser . . . and she was beat up and abused and had black eyes, and stitches and cuts and stuff like this all from her former husband. And before we got married I promised her I wouldn't lay a hand on her which I never have, I never did touch her as far as punch her, not even in playing with her, that set her off. I think it was something like going back into time when she was abused and me raising my voice in the tone of voice that I used kind of scared her (Stamp and Sabourin 1995, 290–91).
>
> I didn't really hit her, I didn't really hit her or nothing, I just threw her down (Stamp and Sabourin 1995, 291).

Minimization was also apparent in *Booth* plaintiff Steven Blake's insistence that the members of R-KIDS had been penalized by the courts for "false or wildly exaggerated claims of 'domestic abuse'" (R-KIDS 1999).

Some batterers minimize their violence by pointing out what they could have done but did not do to the victim or what they would do to a man (Hearn 1998):

I was in control enough because if I wasn't in control enough I would have battered her, do you know what I mean? I hit her, yes, but I didn't—I mean if that had been me in a fight in the pub then it would have been a completely different kettle of fish. If that had been a guy, I'd have been kicking and punching and pulling hair. I'd go on biting and doing whatever I could, but I slapped her and I did toss the table at her, but then all I was trying to do was get her out of the room. I was in control enough not to go that far but the slap was a reaction. It was just a slap. I didn't say, "Right I'm going to hit you." She scratched me and it was almost instantaneous. [She] had a bash on her head where the table had bashed her head and that was all, and a bit of a sore face, but there was no black eye or anything. I had slapped her but nothing—not really badly (Dobash et al. 2000, 15).

I talked to him and said "this is really stupid because I hate to be locked up for a lie. I never was violent. I never hit a woman before in my life. I never have." One time I got mad at her and I pushed her, you know, but other than that I have never, you know, physically hit a woman. And being where I used to box, I wrestled, I practiced martial arts for 11 years. If I wanted to hit her, I would hurt her. So, you know, that taught me discipline not to ever, I don't hit nobody (Stamp and Sabourin 1995, 292–93).

In the army you're trained to kill. You're a trained killer, but it's not brought into the family, well maybe it is, I don't know. I hit her in the face and bruised her eye and cut her lip so I did use force, but not as much as I probably could have. I could have done more damage (Cavanagh et al. 2001, 705).

Some batterers minimize their violence by denying injury even when evidence of it exists. When asked about whether they had injured their partners, batterers responded:

Not really. Pinching does leave bruises. And, I guess slapping. I guess women bruise easily, too. They bump into a door and they'll bruise (Ptacek 1990, 146).

Not injured. She bruises easily (Ptacek 1990, 146).

Yeah, she bruised. Yeah, she bruises easily anyway. If I just squeeze like that, you know, next day she'll get a mark (Ptacek 1990, 146).

She had my handmark on her face but I had been getting ready to go out and it was really cold and I had gloves on so that's what probably made it so bad (Cavanagh et al. 2001, 704).

I never hurt her badly physically. I never cut her or beat her senseless
(Cavanagh et al. 2001, 705).

It's not as if she's a punch bag. I mean I'm not rattling into her . . . they're
no heavy blows or anything like that (Cavanagh et al. 2001, 706).

It doesn't happen every week or every couple of weeks. It's just a very
occasional time, it's happened (Cavanagh et al. 2001, 706).

These minimizations both serve as veiled threats about what the batterer could do next time (Hearn, 1998) and provide the abuser an opportunity to reiterate his capacity for violence and thus to reaffirm his masculinity.

Another form of minimization Hearn (1998) has identified is nominalization—using the term violence as a noun instead of a verb and so effectively obfuscating the abuser's agency. Nominalization in batterer narratives parallels that found in scholarly and news discourses on domestic violence. Hearn also found frequent use of minimizing phrases such as, "I just . . ."; "I only . . ."; and "That was it. . . ." Multiple minimization tactics often appeared together in individual batterer accounts.

Just a slap you know (Hearn, 1998, 119).

She just had some bruising (Hearn, 1998, 119).

We had an argument and I grabbed her by the hair and I hit her and pushed
her and that was it. She hit me over the head with a shoe. Then somebody
phoned the police (Dobash et al. 2000, 14).

I never killed her or anything, but I stabbed her (Hearn 1998, 101).

She had a wee bit of bleeding on her face (Cavanagh et al. 2001, 705).

It's [violence] not really a big part of our lives . . . it was just a wee bruise, just
a wee tiny bruise . . . it was just a wee mishap (Cavanagh et al. 2001, 705).

These statements reveal that some batterers set a very high bar for behavior they would consider violence or abuse. Hearn has pointed out that batterers' frequent use of the phrase "I just" invokes several meanings that serve to minimize the violence itself and the abuser's culpability for it, including *only* (indicating the limited extent of the violence), *exactly* (establishing his version of the incident as definitive), *spontaneously* (as a natural response to her provocation), and *justified* (as if his actions were a kind of justice, not abuse) (Hearn 1998).

Those who have worked with abusers and studied their accounts point out the similarities between abusers' patterns of denial and minimization and those common among alcoholics and addicts (Adams 1989; Bancroft

2002). David Adams has observed that abusers often minimize the extent and frequency of their violence the way that alcoholics minimize the frequency and extent of their drinking. Abusers use favorable comparisons to "brutes who beat their wives every day" to highlight their self-concept as nonabusive. Alcoholics point to worst-case scenarios, like "those who drink bottles of hard liquor on the street," to demonstrate that their own behavior is not a problem (Adams 1989). While carefully pointing out that abuser behavior is not an addiction like alcoholism, Bancroft described other ways that patterns of abuse parallel patterns of addiction—escalation over time, denial, minimization, blaming others for behavior and problems, choosing to affiliate with peers that support current behavior, lying and manipulating to cover up the problem, unpredictable behavior, pitting family members against one another to take the focus off of the abuser, and high rates of return to abuse after "periods of apparent change" (Bancroft 2002).

Excuse

Because abusers rarely admit to the full extent of their violence or take responsibility for their violent actions, excuses and justifications are frequently part of their accounts (Bancroft 2002; Bograd 1988; Coleman 1980; Dutton 1986; Edleson and Tolman 1992; Hearn 1998; Stamp and Sabourin 1995). Hearn wrote, "Excuses and justifications involve the recognition of the violence but the denial of either responsibility (excuses) or blame (justifications). Whilst in some sense excuses and justifications are conceptual opposites, they are in practice sometimes closely interlinked" (1998, 109). Hearn's observation gets at the contradictions that are so often present in batterer accounts. Indeed, batterers often say, in effect, "I did something but it wasn't my fault. And she deserved it anyway." Such sentiments expose the existence of competing and contradictory cultural messages about violence against women. Indeed, Hearn (1998) pointed out that batterers often use excuses to explain their behavior and justifications to explain victims' behavior.

While recognizing how often these two rhetorical devices occur side by side, distinguishing between excuses and justifications highlights different aspects of accounting for violence. Excuses tend to refer to individual-level factors such as past experiences of abuse or drunkenness (Heise 1998). They answer to cultural norms that prohibit violence by providing a reason that the abuser is not responsible for it. Excuses reveal the abuser's recognition that his violence is perceived as wrong by at least some others. Common excuses disavow responsibility for the violence by depicting the man as the object of forces beyond his control, whether internal or external to the batterer (Adams 1989; Bancroft 2002; Hearn 1998). Excuses often externalize violence as due to alcohol, drug use, or job stress (Edleson and Tolman 1992). Batterers also excuse their violence by blaming it on abuse they suffered in the past or on a separate violent self or consciousness over which they claim to have no control (Hearn 1998).

> I literally hit the girl and was strangling her. . . . I wanted to strangle her and I literally were [sic] strangling her but not self-consciously realizing it (Hearn 1998, 96).
>
> Really she bled to death. I didn't even realise I'd stabbed her, it just happened in a split second (Hearn 1998, 101).
>
> And like I jumped up and I grabbed her, which I didn't mean to and I just took a blackout, and I just can't explain it. . . . When I finally came round she was laying on the floor, dead (Hearn 1998, 101).

Abusers also frequently excuse the violence as some sort of accident, sometimes providing elaborate accounts of how a victim happened to hurt herself through no fault of theirs (Mullaney 2007).

> Oh, we got in an argument. She ran up and pushed me and in the process I pushed her back, and as I pushed her, she fell down and took a nasty bump. During the fall, she hit her head on the—and her back on the coffee table. So her getting hurt in the process of falling, a lot of anger came out (Stamp and Sabourin 1995, 293).
>
> Johnny Jacobs told state police that he only intended to scare Claudia by placing the gun to her face and that it was Claudia who caused the gun to discharge accidentally as she moved forward (Websdale 1998, 26).
>
> As I went to jab forward [with a knife], she was sat on the bed you see, and she'd gone to get up, as I went forward the knife had gone in (Hearn 1998, 112).
>
> I didn't kick the door in. It was when I was walking out, I kicked the door, it wouldn't shut. I kicked the door in a temper and when I kicked it the hinges went back and hit her in the face, bust her nose . . . I didn't mean it and she knows that herself, it was pure accident (Cavanagh et al. 2001, 704).

Disavowals are often comprised of a combination of admitting to some action the abuser does not perceive as violent and asserting that the harm resulting from the incident had nothing to do with his actions.

Justification

Drawing upon cultural beliefs about when and how violence against women is reasonable, acceptable, or normal—exceptions to the "never hit a girl" rule—abusers often justify their violence against women. Unlike excuses, which point to individual-level influences on the abuser and his body, justifications tend to point to interpersonal, community, and cultural factors. The justifications batterers use are stories they think others will accept about the violence, stories selected from an archive of circulating stories about men, women, and violence. Batterers, for example, often construe their serious violence against partners as reciprocal or mutual, similar to the representation of violence in *Booth v. Hvass*.

> I got up off, I was sitting on a stool there at the table and uh, she came up to me and she hit me twice with her fist. And with her temper, if she could grab anything she would throw it and I know the next thing was to throw it at me, so I slapped her. All right, well, she lost her balance and she went reeling across and fell on the uh, oh it's really like a wicker basket except they're real sturdy, you can sit on them and everything and she got a real big gash, okay. And so then I sat down on the couch. And she gets up and the first thing that she did is she grabbed the fish sandwich and she threw it at me. (Stamp and Sabourin 1995, 293–94)

Justifications commonly used by abusers include characterizing their violence as self-defense:

> She was trying to tell me, you know, I'm no fucking good and this and that . . . and she just kept at me, you know. And I couldn't believe it. And finally, I just got real pissed and I said wow, you know. I used to think, you're going to treat me like this? You're going to show me that I'm the scum bag? Whack. Take that. And that was my psychology (Ptacek 1990, 144).
>
> It wasn't right for me to slap her. It wasn't unprovoked, you know what I mean? It was almost like she was being an asshole at that particular time. I think for once in her life she realized that, you know, it was her fault (Ptacek 1990, 145).
>
> On some occasions she was the provoker. It didn't call for physical abuse. I was wrong in that. But it did call for something. . . . You know, you're married that long, if somebody gets antagonistic, you want to defend yourself (Ptacek 1990, 145).

> I wouldn't say I was violent, not really . . . if I have [been] she's given me a
> reason to be violent. I'm not just violent for the sake of being violent
> (Cavanagh et al. 2001, 702).

David Adams (1989) argued that what batterers label self-defense is often violent retaliation for disobedience. Adams described how male abusers categorize even very violent acts including strangling, punching, and beating someone up as self-defense and therefore not violence. At the same time, abusers outline a very different standard for their partners' behavior. Many abusers characterize their partner's disagreeable speech as akin to a violent physical attack and justify physical beatings as self-defense against such perceived attacks (Stamp and Sabourin 1995). One study found that more than half of the batterers blamed their partner's aggressive speech for their violence (Coleman 1980, 208).

> Well, she had um gone into just putting me down and characterizing who I
> was in a very derogatory manner, and, you know I tried to wait it out you
> know and listen to her finish but she wouldn't finish. She was just going
> for the jugular, she was going for the kill, going for the you know like she
> just—almost until I would react in some way that she could justifiably
> make me wrong so she could be right (Stamp and Sabourin 1995, 290).
> I have no hesitation about breaking everything in the house. After we calm
> down from the whole story, I get hold of myself and ask myself, what did
> I do? I hurt the person I love, and she hurt me in a different way. The
> woman was humiliated. She will never forget this. Not what she did to
> me and not what I did to her (Eisikovits and Buchbinder 1997, 492).

Many abusers use such reversal to depict themselves as the *real* victim despite the physical harm they have inflicted upon their partner. Although this type of justification often includes explicit claims that their violence was in self-defense, abusers also commonly present their violence as retaliation against a similar harm in order to make their violence seem reciprocal. This kind of representation is also found in news coverage of violence, which tends to describe it as mutual when the woman has used violent resistance or other behaviors deemed inadequately feminine (Adams 1989; Bancroft 2002; Edleson and Tolman 1992; Hearn 1989; McCarthy 1994–95). Many abusers simply feel justified in their use of violence to get what they want:

> I told her: You yelled at me, haggled with me, and lectured me, which you
> should not have done. I hit you, which I should not have done. If you could

just give in, the whole mess could be avoided. (Eisikovits and Buchbinder 1997, 491)

Equating very different kinds of aggression and violence is part of abusers' "account-keeping" mindset (Bancroft 2002). Research on batterers suggests that they often keep a running tab of all the ways they feel their partners have disrespected, disobeyed, or wronged them. Reasoning that they are simply settling accounts, abusers then use these transgressions as justifications for physical violence. For some batterers, this kind of account keeping shades into looking for reasons to use violence: "I started looking for excuses. I'd do anything to get an excuse [to use violence]" (Cavanagh et al. 2001, 710). The pairing of excuses and justifications allows batterers simultaneously to deny their violent intentions and garner support or at least understanding of their violent actions.

Patriarchy in Batterer Narratives

In addition to denying, minimizing, justifying, and excusing their violence, many batterers make reference to patriarchal gender norms. Drawing upon ideas about how they are entitled to receive services and deference from women, many abusers justify their violence by calling attention to their partner's failure to perform in accordance with their ideal of femininity. Abusers refer to core aspects of normative femininity in these accounts and justify their violence by citing their partner's inadequately feminine or receptive sexuality, mothering, wifely duties, and deference. In these cases, abusers present their violence as correction or chastisement of their partner in order to improve her behavior. These accounts hearken back to times when abuse was legally condoned as chastisement and thus suggest that this history is indeed still relevant.

A couple more incidents happened over the next year . . . where I did strike her, and basically for the same reason. I tried making love, and making love, and she couldn't do it (Ptacek 1990, 147).

It was over sex, and it happened I guess because I was trying to motivate her. And she didn't seem too motivated (Ptacek 1990, 147).

I think a lot of it had to do with my frustration of not being able to handle the children. You know, they'd tell me to shut up "You're not going to tell me to shut up." And then [my wife] would tell me, you know, "Let me handle this." I said, "I'm the man of the house." Then we'd start arguing. That's basically what used to happen (Ptacek 1990, 147).

The intent is to have her see it my way. You know, "There's no need for you to think the way you're thinking. And you should see it my way, there's something wrong with you. You're being abusive to me by not seeing it my way" (Ptacek 1990, 147–48).

That was a way I could win. She would know that she had gone too far in asking me something, in constantly probing, requiring me to answer. So that would let her know how hurt or angry I was feeling (Ptacek 1990, 148).

She's kind of—I don't want to say dominating. She's a good mother, she's a good housekeeper, she's an excellent cook. But as far as our relationship goes, the old traditional "man wears the pants in the family," it's a shared responsibility. There's no way that you could say I wear the pants in the family. She's dominating in that sense (Anderson and Umberson 2001, 367).

You ask the guy sitting next to me, the guy that's down the hall. For years they all say, "Bill, man, reach down and grab your eggs. She wears the pants." Or maybe like, "Hey man, we're going to go—Oh, Bill can't go. He's got to ask his boss first." And they were right (Anderson and Umberson 2001, 367).

I should just smack you for the lousy wife you've been (Ptacek 1990, 148).

I was going to go up my buddy's house. We was going to watch the game and shit. I usually don't watch the game, but I figured I'd go up there and watch the game [since] my brother was going to be there. [She said,] "Well, you never spend no time with me." I wasn't worrying about it. So when I started out the door, she got in the way of the door. And usually I don't put my hands on her, *but I told her three times to get the fuck out of the way.* You know what I mean? Because I don't want to hear no shit, and I'm leaving (Mullaney 2007, 241; Mullaney's italics).

It's [violence] not justified, I know, but what she's done basically is causing me to do that like when I come [home] from work and she's never hoovered or dusted the place (Cavanagh et al. 2001, 703).

I'd tell her to, "Shut up," but she disn't [sic] . . . I feel it building up inside me and I tell her either to shut-up or just take what comes [violence] (Cavanagh et al. 2001, 710).

Although contemporary social mores might prevent a man from saying, "Women are inferior to men, and therefore men have a right to control them using violence," an abuser might believe it and act accordingly. Instead of framing his violence as having been about women's inferiority, he might describe it by reference to his victim's status as a "whore" in a virgin/whore dichotomy drawn from patriarchal religions and widely circulated elsewhere. This justification focuses on his prerogative to commit violence against "bad" women, rather than all women, allowing him to reconcile blanket condemnations of violence and the competing, enduring assumption that women "ask for" abuse.

Again, these patterns mirror broader discourses on violence against women. In the criminal justice system, victims are granted disparate support and authority in the courtroom depending on how well they fit stereotypes about deserving victims (Ptacek 1999). In the news, perpetrators receive very different coverage of their crimes based on their membership in privileged or stigmatized groups. In scholarly discourses, obfuscatory language diminishes the connections between structural factors and the nature of abuse. In the case of *Booth*, the plaintiffs and their allies characterized women who report abuse to the police or the courts as angry, vindictive, vengeful, cruel, and willing to lie (R-KIDS 1999).

In each of these cases, a discourse ostensibly intended to condemn and address the problem of violence instead recreates the conditions that allow the violence to continue by feeding the abuser's repertoire and undermining the victim's right to live free from violence.

Learning from the Narratives of Men Who Batter Women

Men's narratives about woman abuse identify numerous contributing factors to violence at multiple levels of the social ecology. While batterers draw upon justifications for violence against women that circulate in popular discourses, they also reveal something about the contours of socially acceptable violence. Batterers' narratives support neither the idea that the marriage license is a "hitting license" (Straus, Gelles, and Steinmetz 1981) nor the claim that hegemonic norms for chivalry proscribe men's violence against women (Brott 1994). Men's accounts of their own violence clearly reveal that women's violence against men is not any more acceptable inside the family than it is outside the family. On the contrary, batterer narratives reveal a very low threshold of tolerance for women's failure to submit to male domination and the fact that many male batterers equate women's defiance with violence against men.

Men who batter and the women they abuse both acknowledge that men's efforts to enforce hegemonic gender norms play a significant role in men's violence. While women who are abused and the men who batter them might disagree about whether the use of violence is justifiable, they often concur that men's belief that they are entitled to enforce feminine roles and defend masculine superiority play a part in men's violence against women. Batterer narratives clearly indicate that patriarchy is a significant contributing and enabling factor in men's violence against women. Batterers invoke hegemonic gendered norms—there are social restrictions on men "hitting girls," but there are also social norms indicating when it is acceptable or necessary to do so—to justify their violence to others. Similarly, the consistency of batterer accounts across locations indicates that social norms engendering men's violence against women are persistent and pervasive.

Batterer narratives suggest that patriarchal peer support for using violence to maintain control of women extends beyond friend and family networks at the interpersonal level to the community and cultural contexts. Whether or not antifeminists choose to acknowledge it, patriarchy is important to the men who use violence against women. Male batterers are aware of norms both enabling violence and stigmatizing it, which suggests that the general proscription against violence competes with patriarchal imperatives to maintain male supremacy. The violence-enabling frames batterers identify are not simply proviolence; instead they are proviolence insofar as violence produces masculinity and preserves entitlement. Batterers draw exculpatory frames for violence from the broader culture, and it is necessary to identify these frames in order to inhibit violence rather than simply declaring that they no longer exist.

Although batterers reference mainstream gender expectations, they simultaneously construct palliative accounts in order to position their actions within the boundaries of normative behavior. Scholars and antiviolence advocates should pay careful attention to both the cultural frames that enable violence against women and those that inhibit it. Only by recognizing both can we hope to decrease the violence. While there is an ongoing need for in-depth research on men who batter women, there is almost no research on perpetrators in other dyads. Until more such research has been undertaken, we cannot hope to understand the nature of different forms of violence against intimates.

Researchers have found other patterns in the ways that men talk about their violence against women. Hearn (1998) has noted that men who batter tend to describe violent acts as individual idiosyncratic incidents, removed both from the broader context of the relationship and their personal character. This pattern mirrors the media and scholarly tendency to decontextualize and depoliticize violence. In their study comparing abuser and victim accounts of violence, Dobash et al. (1998) found that male abusers' accounts of violence tend to be "sparse and abbreviated" compared to female victims' accounts. Dobash et al. also noted that batterer narratives often begin at a point that implicates their partner in the violence and tend to leave out the context leading up to it. Framing the violence as reciprocal or mutual in this way reflects the account of violence provided in *Booth v. Hvass* and other efforts to impose gender-blindness.

The findings that batterers minimize their abusive behavior, blame the victim for their own use of violence, and equate their partners' failure to submit with violence all have serious implications for research. Studies that fail to account for these consistent patterns in batterer narratives are likely to produce inadequate findings. Accordingly, such studies cannot be expected to provide accurate information about the incidence, prevalence, or nature of battering. Likewise, because batterers define many abusive and violent acts as justifiable, defensive, and not violent, studies that simply ask whether violent acts are defensive or offensive are likely to be inadequate for understanding the context, meaning, or motives of violence. Because male batterers frequently blame the women they batter for starting or causing the violence, asking who "initiated the violence" or "hit first" is likewise inadequate to understand context, meaning, or motive. Given what we know about how batterers talk about their violence, scholars and advocates are ill advised to take batterer reports at face value in the context of research, the criminal justice system, or batterer intervention programs. However, batterer accounts still provide a rich source of information about conflicting social norms relevant to studying and preventing violence. Their accounts point to contributing factors at each level of the social ecology.

5 | Sex Differences

> Violence in the home is a frequent occurrence in contemporary
> society . . . the use of force between adults in the home is systematically
> and disproportionately directed at women. Recent interpretations of
> these reports [research on violence, aggression, and conflict tactics] often
> mention the first finding but usually fail to recognize or emphasize the
> direction of the violence and grasp the significance of both of these
> findings.
> —*Dobash and Dobash 1979, 15*

> Straus and Gelles are two of the many researchers who have found
> domestic violence distributed equally between the sexes.
> —*Dunn 1994, 16–17*

> It is categorically false to imply that there are the same number of
> "battered" men as there are battered women.
> —*Gelles 1999*

Debates about the magnitude of sex disparities in violence against intimates reflect ideological differences between scholars in multiple disciplines. These debates are important because they color considerations of the meaning, dynamics, and appropriate responses to violence (Johnson and Ferraro 2000; Renzetti 1994; Schwartz 2000). As Johnson and Ferraro (2000) have pointed out, it is impossible to discuss the research on violence against intimates without acknowledging the disagreements about how to measure and understand it. Calls for consideration of the context and meaning of violence are not new. By all accounts, the historical, cultural, social, and interpersonal contexts of violence against women have been of primary importance since the beginning of the battered women's movement (Dobash and Dobash 1979; Ferraro 1996; Gordon 1988; Martin

1981; Pagelow 1981; Pleck 1987; Schechter 1982; Schneider 2000; Yllö and Bograd 1988). Dobash and Dobash argued in 1979,

> A greater understanding of violence will be achieved through a careful consideration of the nature of the social settings and situations in which it occurs. Investigations that attempt to abstract physical violence out of its social settings and focus primarily on the backgrounds or personal characteristics of individuals are not likely to lead to an elucidation of interpersonal violence. (14)

Thirty years on, this observation is still timely. Efforts to institutionalize individualized and decontextualized understandings of violence continue unabated. Scholars have extensively documented efforts to depoliticize and degender domestic violence (Berns 2001; Klein 1997; Lamb 1991; Lerman 1992).

Claire Renzetti wrote in 1994, "I am dismayed by what I perceive as persistent, though certainly not insurmountable, obstacles to fuller understanding of—and, therefore, the development of more effective responses to—intimate violence," namely "the continuing debate surrounding the question of whether women are as violent as men" (195). Renzetti expressed surprise that some criminologists continued to present feminist perspectives on violence against women as monolithic or advocating a "single factor" perspective on intimate violence; implying that patriarchy is the only cause of men's violence against women and that patriarchy itself is a single factor. She noted, "Many feminists have been among the most vocal critics of one-dimensional models of human behavior, including violent behavior" (196). Renzetti was referring to such claims as those made by Donald Dutton: "during the late 1970s a number of single-factor explanations for male assaultiveness toward women were proffered. These included socio-biology, psychiatric disorders, and patriarchy" (internal citations omitted) (1994, 167). However, feminism's focus on a multiplicity of factors is clear from the most cursory investigation of early and recent research (Miller 1994). Furthermore, patriarchy cannot accurately be described as a single factor.

Susan Schechter's *Women and Male Violence* (1982) was the first comprehensive account of the history of the battered women's movement in the United States. In a section entitled, "Ideological and Personal Diversity within the Movement," Schechter stated that while "feminists in the battered women's movement did not always agree on the meaning or implications of feminism" (44), feminism should be viewed as an umbrella term for a variety of political and ideological orientations advocating equity between the sexes. She observed that none of the approaches these feminists took to woman abuse could be accurately termed "single factor" theories. Battered women's shelters were established because a combination of factors—the gendered interpersonal dynamics of violence, women's lower earning power, and such social and cultural factors as women's primary responsibility for child care, social disapproval of divorce, and police apathy—effectively trap women in abusive relationships (Schechter 1982). Those working in the battered women's movement have emphasized the links between gender, politics, culture, and economics from the beginning and have accordingly called for policies that would allow women to be economically self-sufficient and socially free to leave abusers. From the beginnings of the battered women's movement, antiviolence advocates and scholars argued that multiple factors contribute to violence and that multilayered approaches would be necessary to decrease it.

The feminist emphasis on multifactor ecological models for violence is also evident in more recent publications. A three-volume special issue of the journal *Violence Against Women* on women's use of violence stressed its multiple causes. The editors' introduction states, "We hope that the articles in this issue will help researchers and practitioners alike to think more fully and more complexly about women's use of force and remind them that indeed context is everything. All of the authors in this issue are strong advocates of this perspective" (Bible, Dasgupta, and Osthoff 2002, 1269). It is difficult to see how such a persistent focus on diverse approaches, multiple factors, and contextualization could be construed as a single-factor approach. This kind of misunderstanding of the basic terms of feminism and research labeled as feminist emphasizes the need for scholars and others to be familiar with the body of research they criticize.

Renzetti objected to the idea that criminologists or antiviolence advocates should dismiss or "move beyond" feminist theories in favor of understandings of intimate violence that minimize the importance of gender. As she observed, such suggestions are made based on an understanding of feminism that bears little resemblance to the feminist research (1994, 196). In contrast to antifeminist claims, feminist work on intimate violence has never claimed that patriarchy is the only relevant factor in violence against intimates. Likewise, feminists have not claimed that women are never violent or that men cannot be victims of violence. Instead, as Renzetti has pointed out, feminist perspectives on violence against intimates are characterized by an insistence that gender is one important factor that must be considered as part of a "truly integrated, multidimensional theory of domestic violence causation" (1994, 197). Ironically, it is not feminism but dichotomous, patriarchal gender norms that assign violence and aggression to men and nurturing and passivity to women. Contrary to antifeminist complaints that feminism allegedly "silences" male victims, feminisms' advocacy for greater flexibility in gender actually helped to open a discursive space where it is possible to talk about the fact that men are not invulnerable and that women are not incapable of violence. In addition, much of the research that attempts to improve our understanding of women's use of violence has been produced by feminist scholars.

Despite the progress being made toward the development of integrated, multidimensional models of violence, Renzetti and other scholars have observed that the assertion that women are as violent as men in intimate relationships has been growing louder in some locations (Berns 2001; Collier and Sheldon 2006; Dobash and Dobash 1998; Dobash et al. 1992; Flood 1999; Hearn 1998; Messner 2000; White et al. 2000). Such claims as "Violence against women is clearly a problem of national importance, but has anyone ever asked how often men are beaten by women? The unfortunate fact is that men are the victims of domestic violence at least as often as women" (Brott 1994) are ubiquitous on fathers' rights websites. As in the *Booth* case, these websites frequently name Murray Straus as their primary source. Such claims of sex symmetry—that women are "just as violent as men" or "more violent than men" in intimate relationships—are at the core of *Booth v. Hvass* and other initiatives attacking existing violence legislation and services and exemplify one outcome of decontextualizing violence. The only basis on which to make such claims is to focus on one approach to measuring violence taken out of context. Claims of sex symmetry in violence and the numbers to which they point are not as transparent they may seem. As feminists have repeatedly pointed out, many studies have found both different and similar rates for women and men's violence and aggression between intimates (Dasgupta 2002; DeKeseredy 2000; Dobash et al. 1992; Kimmel 2002; Yllö and Bograd 1988). In order to understand violence against women and men it is essential to understand what these rates do and do not reveal and why various estimates are so different.

Claims that domestic violence is sex-symmetrical are ubiquitous on men's rights, fathers' rights, and other antifeminist websites and are presented as established fact there and in some other locations (Dragiewicz 2008; Menzies 2007; Rosen, Dragiewicz, and Gibbs 2009). These claims are not new. Debates about the pervasiveness and nature of intimate partner violence against women and men have been ongoing since the 1970s. Schechter noted that there were already efforts to degender and depoliticize services for battered women in the early 1970s, when funders suggested that an organization called Women's Advocates choose a "less inflammatory" name (Schechter 1982, 63). Dobash and Dobash also remarked on early efforts to impose gender-blind language in their 1979 book *Battered Wives*.

The scholarly exchanges around the nature of sex differences in violence span more than thirty years and reach beyond the border of the United States, which indicates that the struggle for definitional hegemony is a source of ongoing conflict as well as an international concern (Schwartz and DeKeseredy 1993). Perhaps the best-known exchange began with Suzanne Steinmetz's paper, "The Battered Husband Syndrome," which appeared in a 1977–78 issue of the journal *Victimology*. Based on studies of comic strips, anecdotes about arcane cultural practices, and reports of "conflict tactics," Steinmetz speculated that "husband battering" was more widespread than previously thought. In "The Battered Data Syndrome: A Comment on Steinmetz's Article," which appeared in the next issue of *Victimology*, Elizabeth Pleck, Joseph Pleck, Marilyn Grossman, and Pauline Bart disputed Steinmetz's assertions and challenged her interpretation of the data (1977–78). Despite extensive scholarly critique of Steinmetz's piece and the proliferation of violence research since the late 1970s, the article continues to be the source of talking points, reproduced virtually verbatim, in recent antifeminist commentaries, which normally fail to note Steinmetz's recognition of the "greater severity of physical damage to women making their victimization more visible" and "the male's ability to do more damage during nonhomicidal marital physical fights." "When the wife slaps her husband, her lack of physical strength plus his ability to restrain her reduce the physical damage to a minimum," she observed. "When the husband slaps the wife, however, his strength plus her inability to restrain him result in considerably more damage" (Steinmetz 1977–78, 505).

Steinmetz noted that her paper "is not intended to de-emphasize the importance of providing services to beaten wives, but to increase our awareness of the pervasiveness of all forms of family violence" (1977–78, 507). Her stated goal in publishing the "battered husband" paper was to create an awareness of a culture of violence that called for "changing the attitudes and values of society" rather that what she saw as a disproportionate focus on individual "blame" (Steinmetz 1977–78, 507). Her goal was thus entirely compatible with feminist approaches to violence against intimates. Steinmetz differed with feminism about the importance of gender in the culture of violence that she sought to change. Feminists think gender is a highly relevant factor in the etiology of violence, and Steinmetz, apparently, did not. Her claim that men are less likely to report violence due to the pressure they felt to maintain a masculine image indicates that patriarchal masculinity is a key component of even her own hypothesis that men underreport victimization. Many other exchanges debating the extent to which woman abuse is gendered followed this one in *Victimology*, including entire special issues of journals, smaller series of articles in journals, chapters in textbooks on "current controversies," a government workshop investigating sex differences in violence, and many stand-alone books and articles.[1] Many of these exchanges also received coverage in newspapers, magazines, and websites.

In Canada, antifeminist activists and criminologists deployed allegations of sex symmetry in reaction to the publication of results from two large representative surveys, the Canadian National Survey on Woman Abuse in University/College Dating Relationships (DeKeseredy and Schwartz 1998a) and the Canadian Violence Against Women Survey (Johnson 1996).[2] Some Canadians sought to shift attention away from the results of these studies, which documented high rates of woman abuse, by claiming that "women do it too." DeKeseredy observed that such claims were often backed not by research but by anecdotes about "sensational and statistically infrequent violent crimes committed by a few Canadian women" that are atypical of most violence against intimates (DeKeseredy 1999).

In North America, journalists, not scholars, have written some of the publications that have received the most attention, among them Patricia Pearson's *When She Was Bad: Violent Women and the Myth of Innocence* (1997), in Canada, and Philip Cook's *Abused Men: The Hidden Side of Domestic Violence* (1997), in the United States. These books are sometimes cited in lieu of the research they dismiss, dispute, misrepresent, or fail to acknowledge.

Taken as a body, conversations about sex, gender, and violence reveal competing concerns about the potential harm of leaving gender out as opposed to the potential harm of including gender in discussions of violence against intimates. On one side, scholars insist that sex and gender differences are essential factors to consider in understanding and responding effectively to violence. They thus seek to elucidate the incidence, dynamics, and outcomes of domestic violence in different dyads (Breines and Gordon 1983; DeKeseredy 2000; DeKeseredy and Dragiewicz 2007; DeKeseredy and Schwartz 1998a; Dobash et al. 1992; Flynn 1990; Kimmel 2002; Kurz 1989; Saunders 2002). Such approaches are often labeled feminist regardless of the identification of the author or the inclusion of that term in the research. On the other side, other scholars express concern that feminist scholars' emphasis on gender means only talking about men's violence against women, but failing to consider women's violence against men, and ignoring violence in same-sex couples. These scholars seek to dismiss feminist research on the basis of its insistence on the centrality of gender to understanding violence. The *Booth* plaintiffs drew from this antifeminist research to support their contention that acknowledging sex differences in intimate violence in general and recognizing men's violence against women in particular is damaging to all men.

The *Booth* Plaintiffs' Sources

The *Booth* plaintiffs combined two related claims in their argument that women and men were similarly situated with regard to domestic violence. The first was that "women initiate and carry out physical assaults on their partners as often as men do, that in some situations women may be more prone to violence than men" (Amended complaint 2000, 6). To support this claim, they cited an annotated bibliography (Fiebert 1997). They supported their second claim, that "female violence is, in any event, a major social problem" (Amended complaint 2000, 6), with "Physical Assaults By Wives: A Major Social Problem," Straus's chapter from *Current Controversies on Family Violence* (Straus 1993), which was included in the bibliography. Both claims were central to the legal case because they were the foundation of the assertion that women and men are similarly situated, which is prerequisite to an equal protection challenge. The Fiebert bibliography is widely cited on antifeminist websites as proof that women are as violent as or more violent than men, so critiques of it apply beyond the case. Likewise, Straus is a widely cited source of claims about the mutuality of violence, so critiques of his research also have broad relevance.

Critiques of the research alleging sex symmetry in violence against intimates can be broken down into three main categories—concerns about methodology, concerns about the ability of the research to elucidate the dynamics of violence accurately, and concerns about the outcomes of violence. Methodological critiques address the kinds of samples, who is surveyed, the method of collecting data, what the research instrument measures, whether study findings support research conclusions, and what the studies leave out (DeKeseredy 2000; DeKeseredy and Schwartz 1998b; Dobash et al. 1992; Kimmel 2002; Schwartz 2000). Critiques of the ability of research to explain the dynamics of domestic violence focus on the lack of direct and adequate questioning about motives, the failure to distinguish between different kinds of violence, the failure to collect information on the context and meaning of the violence, and representations of "typical" cases of intimate violence. Concerns about the outcomes of violence include the tendency of some studies to minimize injury and other measures of harm and whether policymakers will use findings appropriately.[3] These areas of concern are overlapping and interrelated. Questions about who is included in a sample have implications for creating research that will be used to make claims about the dynamics and nature of violence. Concerns about the presentation of decontextualized "conflict tactics" as synonymous with battering have implications for policy and service provision. Each of these related areas requires consideration.

"Physical Assaults by Wives: A Major Social Problem" (Straus 1993) illustrates many of the deficiencies in the way research is employed in support of sex-symmetry claims. As the title *Current Controversies in Family Violence* indicates, claims about sex symmetry in intimate violence are highly contested. Still, the *Booth* plaintiffs used the book to support their claim that "an impressive corpus of empirical evidence" shows "the repetitious conclusion . . . that, globally speaking, men and women are guilty of about equal rates of domestic violence" (Appellants' reply to amici curiae 2002, 2) . The *Booth* complaint explains the plaintiffs' inclusion of Straus' chapter and Fiebert's bibliography:

> The purpose of calling it to the attention of this court for judicial notice has been to overcome mid-Victorian fixations by showing domestic violence like alcoholism is a problem shared by men and women. That much seems obvious enough to those familiar with both sides of this phenomenon, but we have nailed the point down so that no credible attempt may be made to deny or minimize this basic fact of life. (Appellants' reply to amici curiae, 3)

Yet the characterization of women and men as perpetrating "about equal rates of domestic violence" *is* widely challenged, both in the very documents cited by the *Booth* plaintiffs and elsewhere. Much of the scholarly criticism of the research cited by those who claim women are as violent as men centers on the misuse of the Conflict Tactics Scales (CTS) (DeKeseredy and Schwartz 1998b). Murray Straus and his colleagues developed the CTS in the 1970s at the University of New Hampshire as a quantitative measure of what Straus has termed "intrafamily conflict" and "family problems" rather than battering or woman abuse in partic- ular (Bograd 1990a; Breines and Gordon 1983; DeKeseredy 2000; De- Keseredy and Schwartz 1998b; Dobash and Dobash 1992; Johnson and Ferraro 2000; Kimmel 2002; Nazroo 1995; Saunders 2002; Straus 1979, 1990b; White et al. 2000). Straus defined conflict in the context of this measure as the tactics used to respond to a conflict of interest (1979). The CTS quantifies conflict tactics, which are defined as methods of manag- ing or responding to conflicts or anger between family members or inti- mate partners (Straus 1979). The CTS is generally used in a self-report survey format, often administered by phone. Respondents are typically asked about conflict tactics they have used or have had used against them during the previous year. The original CTS included thirty-eight multiple- choice questions representing nineteen conflict tactics divided into three categories—reasoning, verbal aggression, and violence. Participants were offered response options ranging from never to more than twenty times. The tactics are designated as either severe or minor based on the authors' assumptions about the seriousness of the acts.

A revised version, the CTS-2, included new items, including sections on sexual assault and injury (Straus et al. 1996). The full CTS-2 includes seventy-eight questions. Scholars often use selected sets of questions rather than the entire CTS-2. Scholars who study violence have frequently used, and extensively criticized, both version of the CTS.

The majority of the research used to support claims that women are as violent as men relies on the CTS. In a review of the annotated bibliog- raphy cited by the *Booth* plaintiffs, Kimmel found that fifty-five of the seventy-nine articles used the CTS (2002). Other literature reviews and commentaries alleging sex symmetry in intimate violence also rely heav- ily on this tool (Archer 2000a; Archer 2000b; DeKeseredy and Schwartz 1998b; Saunders 2002). This is important because although proponents of the sex-symmetry theory of violence claim that there are "many re- searchers who have found domestic violence distributed equally between the sexes" (Dunn 1994), they usually cite only CTS-based studies. Accordingly, it is important to understand what the CTS can and cannot reveal about violence.

In "Physical Assaults by Wives: A Major Social Problem," Straus stated that "women initiate and carry out physical assaults on their partners as often as men do" and repeatedly labelled such assaults a "major social problem" (1993). The *Booth* plaintiffs incorporated virtually identical language into their complaint to support their claim that women and men are similarly situated with regard to domestic violence, thereby necessitating that identical emergency shelter and other services be provided to men and women. However, Straus qualified his claims in important ways that are extremely relevant to, but omitted in, the *Booth* complaint. In fact, Straus observed that the experiences of battered women who call the police for help or flee to a shelter are virtually absent from studies using the CTS in representative community samples. Straus wrote,

> Most of the violence that is revealed by surveys of family problems is relatively minor and relatively infrequent, whereas most of the violence in official statistics is chronic and severe and involves injuries that need medical attention. These two types of violence probably have different etiologies and probably require different types of intervention. (Straus 1993, 77)

Contrary to the *Booth* plaintiffs' suggestion, Straus added that his "family problem" research has found that the "assaults" documented in his CTS-derived data rarely cause injury and are a "major social problem" not because they harm men but because they "help legitimate male violence" and men's "serious assaults" against women (1993, 67). Straus argued,

> Community samples contain very few cases involving severe assaults every week or more often and injury. Men tend to be the predominant aggressors in this type of case, but representative sample studies cannot reveal that, because they include few if any such cases. Ironically, the types of cases that are not covered by community surveys are the most horrible cases and the ones that everyone wants to do something about. However, community surveys can tell us little about what to do about these extreme cases because the samples contain too few to analyze separately. (Straus 1993, 77)

Straus observed that, unlike his research with community samples, studies of cases identified by police and shelters are those which "tend to involve injury or chronic severe assault," which "tends to be a male pattern" (1993, 72). In other words, the Straus chapter the *Booth* plaintiffs cited as evidence that women and men are similarly situated with regard to domestic violence explicitly contradicts that idea. Straus argued that his CTS-based studies with representative community samples cannot be used to design services for battered women or men. Instead, he wrote, "It is essential to have research on clinical samples such as those involved with the police or shelters for battered women in order to have data that do apply to such cases and that therefore provide a realistic basis for programs designed to aid the victims and to end the most serious type of domestic violence" (Straus 1993, 77–78). Nonetheless, the *Booth* plaintiffs repeatedly referred to Straus's work in efforts to discredit the research documenting the repetitious and intimidating nature of woman abuse. For example, they argued,

> Anybody watching the Oprah Winfry [*sic*] show featuring the public admissions of violent women would see how irresponsible such suggestions are. None of the scientists who have exploded the inane myth that men are the brutes and women are the victims would ever agree with such lugubrious nonsense. See, e.g., the observations of Dr. Murray Staus [*sic*] at page A213 of the Appellants' Appendix. (Appellants' reply to amici curiae 2002, 6)

Michael Johnson has pointed out that those women surveyed in Straus and Gelles' 1985 CTS-based National Family Violence Survey (NFVS) who reported assaults by their male partners reported an average of six incidents per year. Johnson noted that in the same study, the thirteen women (out of a total sample of 6,002 adults) who reported violence by male partners and had used shelter services reported an average of 15.3 episodes per year (M. Johnson 1995, citing Straus 1990a). Straus noted that shelter sample studies using the same CTS questions found average frequencies of sixty-five to sixty-eight times per year (Straus 1990a, 84 citing Giles-Sims 1983 and Okun 1986). Johnson reiterated Straus's report that the NFVS identified only four women who reported being assaulted sixty-five times or more (M. Johnson 1995), thus reinforcing Straus's assertion that the sample contains too few cases of the most serious form of battering to be a good source of information about it. According to Johnson, these large differences indicated that studies of different populations were probably measuring different phenomena. Johnson called the relatively infrequent, noninjurious forms of intimate violence documented by Straus "common couple violence." He termed the kind of ongoing battering documented by shelters "patriarchal terrorism" (Johnson 1995). In other words, so-called "representative" sample surveys may include a representative sample from the perspective of statistical analysis. However, they mostly capture common couple violence and omit patriarchal terrorism. The reasons for the low response to the NFVS by battered women (survivors of patriarchal terrorism) are unclear, especially in view of the fact that other representative sample surveys have found much higher response rates, even on the same items. However, it is clear that the NFVS found only four women reporting the average number of assaults reported by shelter samples and only thirteen women who had used shelter services. In other words, the very population likely to be affected by lawsuits against shelters and services targeting battered women is virtually absent from the Straus study cited by the *Booth* plaintiffs.

Straus explicitly argued that "the controversy over assaults by women" has resulted in large part from inappropriate generalizations from one kind of research and sample to another. Straus described the "clinical fallacy," which allegedly generalizes from findings based on severely abused women to the general population, and the "representative sample fallacy," which makes generalizations about battering based on "community samples" (1993, 77). However, Straus himself seemed to commit the "representative sample fallacy" throughout "Physical Assaults by Wives: A Major Social Problem" by stressing the idea that women's minor assaults (identified in his sample) lead to men's severe assaults against women (largely absent from his sample). Moreover, Straus and Gelles have published contradictory interpretations of their own CTS-based research, and these interpretations have been repeatedly and selectively quoted on the antifeminist websites linking to the *Booth v. Hvass* documents.

Straus and Gelles's interpretations of their research have shifted so profoundly over time that Martin Schwartz and Walter DeKeseredy wrote an article tracking the changes (Schwartz and DeKeseredy 1993). Early Straus and Gelles publications stressed that women are not as violent as men, that much of women's violence is defensive, and that given the marked sex disparities in injurious violence the majority of resources and attention should be focused on battered women. Their later publications reduce these points to parenthetical statements in favor of overt attacks against feminist scholars and the insistence that men cannot stop their violence if women do not change their behavior first (Schwartz and DeKeseredy 1993).

In addition to the hypothesized clinical vs. representative community sampling issues and the selective attention paid to research limitations, there are other methodological concerns to consider. Research shows that when surveyed about violence they have perpetrated or experienced, men report less violence than women do (Hearn 1998; Szinovacz 1983). Despite women's tendency to report more violence than men, both women and men have been shown to underreport their actual experience of violence (Dobash and Dobash 1998; Edleson and Brygger 1996; Jouriles and O'Leary 1985, Szinovacz 1982). Although antifeminist authors speculate that men are less likely than women to report violence in crime surveys and other contexts, the review of the limited available research by Dobash and colleagues (Dobash et al. 1992) indicates the opposite. Men who are assaulted by intimates are actually more likely to call the police, more likely to press charges, and less likely to drop them (76). Similarly, Schwartz found that among those injured by intimates men were slightly more likely than women to report the incident to police (1987, 66–67).

Research Demonstrating Sex Differences in Violence against Intimates

The research demonstrating women's grossly disproportionate risk from violence perpetrated by male intimates is often obscured when our attention is focused on a small subset of survey research dealing with the incidence and prevalence of decontextualized acts. Regardless of the reason for this artificially narrow focus, claims based on such a limited portion of the research distort the realities of violence until it bears no meaningful relationship to the experiences of batterers or survivors. The word "symmetry" denotes balance, exact correspondence, and equivalence, which even the sources cited in support of symmetry claims fail to support. Symmetry claims can be made only when research on the negative outcomes of intimate violence is ignored (Dragiewicz and Lindgren 2009, 245). Although *Booth v. Hvass* made reference to "severe assaults" as Straus arbitrarily defined them, the lawsuit completely ignored research on homicide, separation assault, sexual assault, stalking, injury, and other outcomes. These types of violence are arguably most pertinent to establishing need for emergency shelter and the proportionality of risk for women and men.

Homicide

Homicide is the most serious form of intimate violence. The research on homicide rates avoids many of the definitional problems endemic to the study of sublethal violence and is also more reliable than research on sublethal violence because it does not rely on self-reports (Garcia et al. 2007). Homicide is also much more likely to be reported than sublethal violence. "Homicide is of interest not only because of its severity but also because it is a fairly reliable barometer of all violent crime," the Bureau of Justice Statistics report *Homicide Trends in the United States* observes. "At a national level, no other crime is measured as accurately and precisely" (Fox and Zawitz 2010).

Data collection on basic demographic variables related to homicide is conducted through the Federal Bureau of Investigation's Supplementary Homicide Reporting (SHR) program. SHR data includes such factors as the age, sex, and race of victims and perpetrators, any weapon used, and the number of perpetrators per incident. The SHR form also includes a space for recording the circumstances of the homicide, including the relationship between victim and offender (Federal Bureau of Investigation 2004).

The SHR data have some limitations that are relevant to understanding domestic homicide. For example, it is not mandatory that law enforcement agencies complete the forms, so not every homicide is included. Contextual details are often sparse or missing from the completed forms. In addition, the SHR form includes codes for current and former husbands and wives but not for former girlfriends, boyfriends, or common-law partners. As a result, SHR records underestimate the total number of domestic homicides. For example, a Michigan study using multiple data sources to identify domestic homicides found 34 percent more domestic homicides than those identified by the SHR alone (Biroscak et al. 2006, 393). This is a significant difference. Despite its limitations, the SHR is the most frequently cited source of official statistics on homicide (Biroscak et al. 2006, 393).

SHR homicide data reveal profound sex differences.[4] At the national level, statistics using the SHR data have consistently documented women's disproportionate risk of being killed by a current or former intimate partner. In 2005, 33.3 percent of female homicide victims were killed by intimates and 2.5 percent of male homicide victims were killed by intimates (Fox and Zawitz 2010). Of the 1,510 people killed by intimates in 2005, 329, or approximately 22 percent, were men, and 1181, approximately 78 percent, were women. Intimate-partner homicides of men declined 75 percent between 1976 and 2005 (Fox and Zawitz 2010), but while they have been rapidly decreasing as a proportion of all homicides of men intimate-partner homicides of women have remained about a third of all homicides of women during this period (Fox and Zawitz 2010). Aggregated homicide numbers show an overall decrease in intimate-partner homicides between 1976 and 2005 but obscure significant differences by race: the number of black men killed decreased 83 percent, the number of white men killed dropped 61 percent, the number of black women killed decreased 52 percent, and the number of white women killed by intimates decreased 6 percent (Fox and Zawitz 2010). Aggregate statistics also obscure differences in changes in the rate of homicides by relationship type, with intimate-partner homicides of spouses decreasing much more than homicides of girlfriends and boyfriends since 1976 (Fox and Zawitz 2010).

While Minnesota does not have a statewide fatality review process, its first statewide report on homicide was available when *Booth v. Hvass* was being prepared (Erickson 1999). According to that report, approximately eight of ten victims of intimate-partner homicide were women between 1985 and 1997 (15). That statistic reveals marked sex differences, but it does not tell the whole story. Because the Minnesota report was based on SHR data, the methodological weaknesses of SHR also apply to the state report.

Research on the dynamics of intimate-partner homicide that has gone beyond simple rates and demographics brings sex differences into sharper relief.[5] Margot Wilson and Martin Daly noted that the sex ratio of female to male intimate-partner homicides was closer in the United States than in any other country between 1976 and 1985, but that the ratio was so close did not, they argued, "imply symmetry in wives' and husbands' actions or motives" (1992, 206). Since 1985, the sex ratio of intimate-partner homicides in the United States has diverged and come to resemble more closely the sex differences in other countries (Fox and Zawitz 2010). In a 2007 review of the current research, Jacqueline Campbell and her colleagues observed that the rate of intimate-partner homicides of women is four to five times higher than that for men (2007, 246). Campbell and colleagues noted, "The most important risk factor of [intimate-partner] homicide identified to date is [intimate-partner violence] against the female partner with approximately 67 percent to 75 percent of [intimate-partner] homicides with a reported history of [intimate-partner violence] against the female partner, no matter which partner is killed" (Campbell et al. 2007, 253). In other words, a history of men's violence against women is the most common precedent for intimate partner homicides of women *and* men.

Russell Dobash, R. Emerson Dobash, Margo Wilson, and Martin Daly emphatically summarized the sex differences in intimate-partner homicide in 1992:

> Men often hunt down and kill a spouse who has left them; women hardly ever behave similarly. Men kill wives as part of planned murder-suicides; analogous acts by women are almost unheard of. Men kill in response to revelations of wifely infidelity; women almost never respond similarly, although their mates are more often adulterous. Men often kill wives after subjecting them to lengthy periods of coercive abuse and assaults; the roles in such cases are seldom if ever reversed. Men perpetrate familial massacres, killing spouses and children together; women do not. Moreover, it seems clear that a large percentage of the spousal killings perpetrated by wives, but almost none of those perpetrated by husbands, are acts of self-defense. Unlike men, women kill male partners after years of suffering physical violence, after they have exhausted all available sources of assistance, when they feel trapped, and because they fear for their own lives. (81)

These observations are robustly supported by the extant research on intimate-partner homicide. Nancy Jurik and Russ Winn found that "compared to men, women more frequently kill intimates and kill in situations in which their victim initiated the physical aggression" (1990, 227). While women are much less often the perpetrator in homicides, a greater proportion of female-perpetrated homicides are against partners or are defensive than is the case for male-perpetrated homicides. In her sample of women who killed intimates in Chicago, Ann Goetting found that approximately 56 percent of the cases were victim-precipitated (1988, 12). Goetting noted that this is a higher proportion than the percentage of victim-precipitated cases in nonintimate homicides, which indicates different etiologies for intimate and nonintimate homicides as well as for women's and men's homicides. Laura Dugan, Daniel Nagin, and Richard Rosenfeld posited that the sharp decline in male homicide victimization by female partners in recent years is likely due to the increased availability of resources to assist women in escaping men's violence in the United States (1999). Rosenfeld also argued that women's ability to divorce, in combination with the availability of domestic violence services, contributed to the significant decline in intimate homicides of men (Rosenfeld, 1997). Angela Browne and Kirk Williams argued that given the sex differences in intimate-partner homicide declines since the 1970s theories that fail to account for gender are simply not viable (1993).

Sex differences in intimate-partner homicide are brought further into focus when homicide-suicides are added to the picture. Counts of deaths due to intimate-partner homicide can easily obscure the nature of these crimes and the identities of the perpetrators, especially in multiple killings. Although the federal government does not maintain a national database on homicide-suicide, studies that have investigated homicide-suicides have found them to comprise a significant portion of intimate homicides (Fawcett, Starr, and Patell 2008; Fukuroda 2005; Harper and Voigt 2007). The Violence Policy Center found that intimates perpetrated 73 percent of murder-suicides in the United States in 2007. Of murder-suicides of intimates, 94 percent were perpetrated by men against women (2008, 5). In Dee Wood Harper and Lydia Voigt's study of forty-two homicide-suicides in New Orleans from 1989–2001, thirty were intimate-partner homicides, and twenty-nine were perpetrated by men against women (303). Studies of intimate homicide-suicide link it to patriarchal and proprietary control of women (Daly and Wilson 1988; Easteal 1993; Websdale 1999).

Familicide, when a person kills an intimate partner and one or more children in the family, is another important variation of intimate homicide. Familicide is "virtually a male monopoly" as more than 90 percent of perpetrators are male (Wilson et al. 1995, 279–80). In their study of familicide in Canada, England, and Wales between 1974 and 1990, Margo Wilson, Martin Daly, and Antoinetta Daniele found 93 percent of Canadian familicides and 96 percent of English and Welsh familicides to be male-perpetrated (1995, 280). In an earlier study of Canadian homicide records between 1961 and 1983, Wilson and Daly found sixty-one cases where a man killed his female partner and one or more children and no cases where a woman had killed a partner and child (1988, 82.). Local homicide reviews find similar patterns of nearly universal male perpetration in familicide (Fawcett et al. 2008; Fukuroda 2005; Harper 2007).

Overall, the research on every form of intimate homicide finds marked sex differences, with the vast majority of intimate-partner homicides perpetrated by men against women. The different dynamics of women's and men's intimate-partner homicides point to an even greater difference than that indicated by the body counts alone. These differences are directly relevant to the provision of services tailored to the needs of battered women, especially given that existing services are inadequately funded and forced to turn away many of the women who ask for help. Because the prevention of homicide is a compelling state interest to which domestic violence shelters bear a direct relationship, the homicide data are pertinent to equal protection claims. As the most serious form of violence against intimates, the research on homicide must be accounted for in any reasonable claims about the nature and distribution of violence.

Separation Assault

Scholars and others who make claims that domestic violence is sex symmetrical normally ignore the research on separation assault. While the availability of divorce and domestic violence-related services has increased the possibility of separating from abusers and is thus thought to have decreased the risk of intimate homicide, especially for men, separation does not automatically end the risk of violence (DeKeseredy and Schwartz 2009; Rosenfeld 1997). The research on separation and divorce assault contributes to the understanding of violence and abuse by highlighting the violence that is deployed during and after separation, often as a part of efforts to maintain or regain control of women who are trying to leave (DeKeseredy at al. 2004; DeKeseredy and Schwartz 2009; Hardesty 2002; Kurz 1996).

Information on rates of separation assault is limited because of definitional issues in research and reporting on violence and abuse (DeKeseredy and Schwartz 2009). Research reports often combine rates for current and former partners, and most research does not assess the chronology of assaults. This makes it difficult to discern such factors as whether research reports on stalking refer to acts perpetrated by former or current partners (Tjaden and Thoennes, 1998). However, the available data has found sex-asymmetrical violence by former partners, with American men more likely than women to assault, stalk, rape, and kill partners after separation (Catalano 2007; 1995; Tjaden and Thoennes 1998; Websdale 1999; Wilson and Daly 1993).

A review of intimate-partner homicides in the United States between 1976 and 1995 found that women were more than twice as likely as men to have been killed by a former spouse (Puzone et al. 2000, 414). James Alan Fox and Marianne Zawitz found that between 1976 and 2005 former spouses were the perpetrators in 1.4 percent of homicides of women and .2 percent of homicides of men in the United States (2010). In their study of spousal homicides reported to the police in Canada (1974–90), New South Wales, Australia (1968–86), and Chicago, Illinois (1965–90), Wilson and Daly found that women who were estranged from their husbands

were more likely to be killed by them than women who were not estranged from their husbands. Wilson and Daly noted, "Wives are much
more likely to be slain by their husbands when separated from them than
when coresiding. Coresidency status does not appear to have a similar
bearing on the risk to husbands" (1993, 8). Based on National Crime Victimization Survey (NCVS) data from 2001 to 2005, Shannan Catalano
found that, per thousand persons aged twelve and older, rates of annual
nonfatal victimization by intimate partners were 10.4 for divorced women,
2.6 per for divorced men, 40.7 for separated women, and 12.8 for separated
men (2007).

Ruth Fleury, Cris Sullivan, and Deborah Bybee found that half of the
women they interviewed over two years after they had left a battered
women's shelter were not reassaulted (2000, 1381). However, several studies indicate that for many women separation may be a time of increased
risk from abusive men. Fleury et al. found that more than one-third of
the women in their study of women who had used a battered women's
shelter were reassaulted within two years of leaving the shelter (2000,
1636). Ronet Bachman and Linda Saltzman found that women separated
from husbands were three times more likely to have been assaulted than
women who were divorced and twenty-five times more likely to have
been assaulted than married women (1995, 4).

These statistics are highly relevant to *Booth v. Hvass* because those
seeking shelter have by definition left the abuser, if only temporarily.
Shelters exist to prevent violence by the abuser after the victimized partner attempts to leave the household, as well as to provide a place to go
when there is no other option. As research shows, intimate partners requiring this type of protection are overwhelmingly female.

Stalking

According to Tjaden and Thoennes, stalking is "a course of conduct directed at a specific person that involves repeated visual or physical proxim-
ity, nonconsensual communication, or verbal, written or implied threats,
or a combination thereof, that would cause a reasonable person fear"
(1998, 5). They found women four times more likely to be stalked in their
lifetime than men (2–3) and more likely to be stalked by intimates; of all
women who were stalked, 59 percent were stalked by intimates, while of
all men stalked 30 percent were (5–6). Eighty-seven percent of identified
stalking perpetrators are men, and 78 percent of victims are women (5).

In 94 percent of cases with female stalking victims, the perpetrators were men (5). Seventy-nine percent of women who were stalked by an intimate were stalked after breaking up with that intimate (8). Eighty-one percent of women who were stalked by an intimate were also physically assaulted by them, and 31 percent were raped by them (8). Tjaden and Thoennes found stalking linked to higher rates of physical and sexual assault by male perpetrators: men who stalked female partners were four times likelier to assault them physically and six times likelier to rape them than perpetrators who did not stalk (8). Thus, while stalking is experienced by both women and men, it also displays marked sex asymmetry.

Sexual Assault

Whether perpetrated by intimates, acquaintances, or strangers, women are at much greater risk of sexual assault than men. National studies offer conservative estimates of the prevalence of rape. A 1993 review of published research on the prevalence of rape in the United States found estimates of the number of women who would be raped in their lifetimes ranging from 2 percent to 24 percent (Koss, 200). The National Violence Against Women Survey (NVAWS) found 17.6 percent of women and 3 percent of men had experienced attempted or completed rape (Tjaden and Thoennes 1998, 3). In the same study, 7.7 percent of women and 0.3 percent of men reported having been raped by a current or former intimate partner (Tjaden and Thoennes 2000, 26). The NCVS found that the rates of men reporting sexual assault were too small to analyze statistically, but 96 percent of rape victims in the study were women and 4 percent were estimated to be men (Rennison 2002, 1).[6] The majority of sexual assaults are not reported to police (Rennison 2002, 3). In their review of the research on separation and divorce sexual assault, DeKeseredy et al. found rates ranging from 6 to 60 percent based on the sample, research method, and time period covered by the studies (2004, 681). Because sexual assault is regularly reported as part of the continuum of violence and abuse men use against female intimate partners, literature reviews that omit sexual assault cannot be considered valid or complete representations of woman abuse.

Sublethal Injury

Although often reduced to a parenthetical aside in sources alleging sex symmetry in violence, sublethal injury is an essential factor to consider in studying violence. Injuries perpetrated by intimates comprise a greater portion of all injuries to women than to men (Rand 1997, p.1). A 1997 study of violence-related injuries treated by United States emergency departments found that 37 percent of women and 5 percent of men had been injured by a former or current intimate partner (Rand 1997, 5). Schwartz has noted that scholars have paid more attention to incidence and prevalence rates for spousal assault than to the severity of violence (1987, 62). Studies on the prevalence of sublethal violence often omit sex differences in injuries or explain them as accidental outcomes of men's larger size.

Alternatively, some scholars have reported similar rates of injury of women and men in cases where they were physically attacked (Steinmetz, 1977–78). Schwartz (1987) explained this alleged similarity in injuries to women and men from spouses by noting that while rate of injury was similar among those physically attacked by a spouse, women are more likely to be attacked by a spouse; thus intimates injure more women than men (1987). Kevin Strom's study of injury based on the National Electronic Injury Surveillance System, which is a representative sample of United States emergency departments, found that 84 percent of those injured but not killed by intimates were women (2000, 1). At the same time, Strom's study found that a larger portion of the injuries to men (68 percent) than women (19 percent) were caused by a weapon (1). Overall, Strom's study indicated that of the 243,400 people who sought treatment in a U. S. emergency department for intentional injuries inflicted by a partner, 204,400 were women (Strom 2000, 9). Although the minority of male victims were more likely to have been injured by a weapon than by their partner's body, women were much more likely to be injured (13).

Implications of Sex Differences in Violence against Intimates

Claims about sex symmetry in violence against intimates are not supported by the research when the multiple relevant types and measures of violence are considered. While sex differences speak to differential risks from intimate partners for women and men, incidence and prevalence estimates tell us very little about the nature of violence and abuse. A narrow focus on numbers of women and men who have ever been aggressive or violent directs attention toward individual women and men and away from the contexts that produced their behavior.

In addition, the myopic focus on sex as a demographic category obscures profound differences in rates of violence across such categories as race, class, and marital status (Bureau of Justice Statistics 2007; Federal Bureau of Investigation 2004). Differences in the prevalence of violence against and by women and men across demographic categories are extremely well documented. Research is needed to investigate the specific dynamics of violence—its meaning for those involved, its outcomes including but not limited to death and injury, and the contexts in which it takes place. The assertion that women's and men's violence is essentially similar simply because both female and male perpetrators and victims exist is absurd.

In addition to becoming aware of the critiques of research used to make claims about sex symmetry and reviewing research that documents sex asymmetry, readers might consider why some scholars and fathers' rights groups are so quick to dismiss the information provided by battered women, feminists, shelters, hospitals, police, lawyers, batterers, criminologists, and others in order to embrace statistics that ostensibly show sex symmetry. Dobash et al. argued that dismissing this evidence in favor of relying on CTS-based findings of "symmetry" is tantamount to "assuming that [CTS] questionnaire data have a validity that battered women's injuries and deaths lack" (Dobash et al. 1992, 80). One place to look for information about why anyone would make symmetry claims given the copious evidence of sex asymmetry is in recommendations about what should be done with this data. *Booth v. Hvass* urged that funding for domestic violence services be eliminated, sex differences and the role of gender in violence be ignored, and knowledge that can be construed as feminist be dismissed. These recommendations point to goals other than decreasing the violence.

This chapter has focused narrowly on the most conservative estimates of violence and abuse—mostly those documented in public reports of crimes and physical violence. This small subset of violence and abuse is the tip of the iceberg. Many scholars have recounted battered women's reports that psychological abuse is one of the most damaging aspects of woman abuse. Antifeminists use this observation to minimize the importance of physical violence against women and insinuate that women are "as violent as men" when psychological abuse is taken into account. However, scholars and policymakers need to be cognizant of the big picture. Psychological abuse must be considered in the larger context of credible threats of physical violence.

6 | Gender and Patriarchy

A critical point is that even if women were as aggressive as men (a point not yet proven), partner violence is still not a gender-neutral phenomenon. In a society organized socially and psychologically along the lines of gender, aggression and violence among male and female partners are necessarily gendered in the meaning of the experience, provocations, and consequences.
—*White et al. 2000, 694*

No one denies that wives can be violent or that some husbands are battered. Incidence rates are not the issue. Rather, the question is whether gender is useful to our understanding of battering.
—*Bograd 1990b, 134*

Although studies quantifying sex differences receive a disproportionate amount of media attention, they comprise only a small portion of the total research on human violence, most of which investigates the social and structural factors that can potentially be changed in order to reduce violence. One issue highlighted by such lawsuits as *Booth v. Hvass* and the discourses surrounding them is the conflation and confusion of the terms sex, gender, and patriarchy.

The issue of how gender is relevant to violence is salient regardless of the existence of contradictory claims about the magnitude of sex differences. It is important to talk about gender as well as sex because violence against intimate partners exhibits both sex differences and gender differences. Gendered social practices and institutions contribute to the observed sex differences in violence, just as they do to other kinds of human behavior. Understanding gender differences helps answer questions about how and why violence happens. Gender and other social and structural differences are also important to making decisions about where and how to expend scarce resources for violence prevention and intervention.

Opponents of gender-inclusive analyses of violence frequently ask two questions—"How can domestic violence be a gender issue if women and men are both sometimes violent?" and "How can domestic violence be a gender issue if it happens in same-sex couples?" Such questions are based on the incorrect conflation of the concepts of sex and gender.

Gender

The terms sex and gender are often used interchangeably. Some applications and forms, for example, often include a box for identifying one's "gender" as female or male; others identify these as "sex" categories. Most people, scholars and nonscholars alike, use these terms interchangeably in everyday conversation. Jayde Pryzgoda and Joan Chrisler's study of understandings of the word gender found, "When psychologists describe something as gendered or talk about gender differences, there is about a 50% chance that readers will assume that they are referring to sex and about a 50% chance that readers will question what they mean" (2000, 300–301). While the word gender is used more frequently than in the past, this finding indicates that understanding of the conceptual difference between sex and gender is still limited. In addition, the exact boundaries of the concept of gender are still evolving.

The social sciences have recognized sex and gender as distinct concepts for many years, and the fields of human rights, public health, and medicine are increasingly coming to the same understanding (American Medical Association 2000; Fishman et al. 1999; Johnson, Greaves, and Repta 2009; Phillips 2005). The particular usage of these terms has changed over time and varies somewhat across contexts. Jennifer Fishman, Janis Wick, and Barbara Koenig have argued that "careless usage of 'gender' in the biomedical literature leads to misinterpretation and imbues the reported research results with unintended meanings" (1999, 16). While it may be inadvertent, this lack of care in the use of language has "serious implications for future research, clinical practice and treatment, as well as our very understanding of the nature of the health outcomes and status differences that we are studying" (Fishman et al. 1999, 15).

Fishman and colleagues note that while the medical field is just beginning to grapple with the notion of a sex/gender distinction, social scientists are already complicating the concept as they puzzle out how sex, gender, gender identity, and sexuality interact with one another. The question of where sex ends and gender begins is more complex than it might seem. Indeed, medical researchers have noted the complicated interaction of biology and culture and pointed to the difficulty of drawing a clear line where biology ends and culture begins. There is a need for further theoretical and empirical research to explore these categories and the correspondences between them.

Despite these difficulties, the failure to distinguish between sex and gender has a high cost. The conceptual distinction between sex and gender is a valuable one that can be used to disentangle biological and social contributions to human behavior, health, and social problems. Distinguishing between biological and social factors can improve our understanding of human violence in order to prevent it better. As Jackson Katz has noted in his commentary on responses to the film *Tough Guise*,[1] many people still believe that men are more violent than women because of inherent biological differences (Katz and Jhally 2009). However, remarkable variation in rates of violence across time and location indicate that there is much more than biology at work. Deepening our understanding of the ways in which gender and other social and structural factors shape violence is a necessary step toward strategizing about how to reduce and respond to it effectively.

The distinction between sex and gender provides a useful analytical framework for analyses of human behavior. Although sex is most often considered to be a given, gender is clearly culturally constructed and therefore open to the possibility of changes that would broaden the range of acceptable attributes and behavior for women, men, girls, and boys. This broadening of possibilities is one of the central goals of feminism. The refusal to recognize or acknowledge the sex/gender distinction, on the other hand, is a tactic that can be used to naturalize existing gender roles and foreclose the possibility of change.

In the most simplified terms, "sex" refers to the biological categories female and male. Traditionally, sex is assigned on the basis of the appearance of a baby's genitals at birth. If the baby's genitals are ambiguous, the baby's sex may be assigned after investigation of the baby's internal anatomy or chromosomes. Babies that do not appear to fall clearly into the typical female or male sex categories at birth are referred to as intersex. Some individuals are also discovered to be intersex later in life, such as at puberty. "Intersex is a socially constructed category that reflects real biological variation," according to the Intersex Society of North America

(ISNA), rather than a category that is discrete or naturally occurring (ISNA 2009). As ISNA explains, different doctors may have different opinions about the specific boundaries of the categories female, male, and intersex. Still, sex typically refers to the binary, biologically based categories female and male.

"Gender," on the other hand, refers to the socially constructed categories feminine and masculine, which are normatively associated with women and men. Expression of gender varies across cultures and over time. Some gender norms have become less restrictive in recent years; it is, for example, no longer uncommon to see women wearing pants or going to law school. However, gender norms continue to exert a powerful pressure in many, if not most, areas of social life. Everything from how we walk and dress to how we interact with others is influenced by gender norms. These norms are so commonplace and taken for granted that we are likely not to notice them until we experience something out of the ordinary. For example, in travelling to another country, North Americans might be surprised to see male friends holding hands or women who do not shave their armpits. Social rules for touching and hair removal are both gendered and normative; that is to say, observing deviation from the norm is likely to be accompanied by a judgment about the moral or social meaning of the behavior.

In addition to shaping our behaviour in both conscious and unconscious ways, gender is an important conceptual category that people use to organize their interactions with others. The *Saturday Night Live* character Pat, played by actor Julia Sweeney, provides one illuminating example from popular culture. Pat's androgynous appearance is a source of confusion and frustration for Pat's coworkers, who try to devise questions that will solve the riddle of Pat's sex. Pat illustrates the strangeness of meeting a person who cannot be linked by their performance of gender to their sex and reflects the common mental imperative to categorize each person we meet according to sex, just as we do for age and race. These judgments are usually unconscious, so the occasional failure of categorization has the potential to reveal how assumptions about sex and gender deeply influence our interactions on an ongoing basis. Marilyn Frye has written,

> Sex-identification intrudes into every moment of our lives and discourse, no matter what the supposedly primary focus or topic of the moment is. Elaborate, systematic, ubiquitous and redundant marking of a distinction

between two sexes of humans and most animals is customary and obligatory. One *never* can ignore it. (1983, 19)

Daytime talk shows provide many more examples of this phenomenon, with such television personalities as Maury Povich hosting episodes where the audience is asked to discern a person's sex from his or her appearance and comportment: are the guests "babes" or "hunks?" Other episodes include guests revealing their sex on camera to people who thought they were the "opposite" sex, thus inviting the audience to participate vicariously in surprise, anger, and revulsion. These examples from popular culture reveal that although they are often unconscious, assumptions about the relationship between sex and gender are deeply ingrained in our thinking and perceptions, so much so that interruptions to these associations are surprising or upsetting. The English language, which lacks a commonly used sex- or gender-neutral pronoun, makes it tricky even to write about androgynous people in a way that is grammatically correct. Although gender-neutral pronouns like "ze" and "hu" have been proposed and are used in some circles, they have not caught on and are rarely utilized.

In addition to being linked to sex, gender norms are also closely linked to heteronormativity (Pharr 1987; Rich 1980). It is largely assumed until there is reason to believe otherwise that women will have male intimate partners and men will have female partners. Failure to conform comes at a cost. Adrienne Rich described heterosexuality as "compulsory." Rich wrote, "Lesbian experience is perceived on a scale ranging from deviant to abhorrent" (1981, 632). In other words, lesbianism is not just different from heterosexuality; it is culturally constructed as inferior. Those who fail to perform hegemonic gendered traits well enough often confront such homophobic slurs as "fag" and "dyke" regardless of their sexuality as well as violence up to and including homicide. Rich argued that due to the real and pervasive pressures toward heterosexuality and the penalties for failing to perform it, heterosexuality could be described as imposed or coerced rather than inherent, preferred, or freely chosen. Suzanne Pharr (1987) has argued that homophobia and sexism are inextricably intertwined. Millett (1969) observed that while sex, gender, and sexuality may be positioned in a sort of conceptual Venn diagram with distinct and overlapping areas, the associated sex, gender, and sexual categories are concurrently in a hierarchical relationship with one another. Sex and gender are labels that can be used to create categories, but they alone do not sufficiently address power relations. While heteronormativity points to the hierarchical relationship between heterosexuality and homosexuality, patriarchy indicates the hierarchical relationship between women and men.

Patriarchy

Feminist critiques of violence stress the importance of patriarchy as a contributing factor. When opponents of gender-inclusive research ask, "How can domestic violence be about patriarchy if women are also perpetrators?" and "How can domestic violence be about patriarchy if it happens in same-sex couples?" they confuse and conflate patriarchy and sex, as they apparently equate patriarchy with heterosexual men. However, "patriarchy" does not simply denote "men," nor does it affect only men. Patriarchy is not a single factor that is inherent in a single man or in the dynamics of a single man's heterosexual relationship (Walby 1990). Likewise, patriarchy is not simply a synonym for sexism. Patriarchy is a socioeconomic system that generally privileges and values men over women and masculinity over femininity (Johnson 2005).

In patriarchal cultures, rigid, polarized, and hierarchical gender roles work to maintain a strong, normative relationship between sex and gender. Shifting gender roles has the potential to call into question the power relations between women and men, as they too are revealed to be constructed and therefore changeable. While a more equitable distribution of power, rights, resources, and status is desirable from feminist perspectives, those who want to maintain existing power relations reject such changes. One way to undermine the threat of feminism's critiques of patriarchy is to deny that gender is socially constructed, thus naturalizing gendered hierarchies of power and making changes to them appear undesirable, if not impossible. Often, antifeminist writers claim that asserting a role for gender in shaping violence is "going too far" and denies men their rights. In fact, feminist analyses call for equal access to power and authority, which includes challenging the male privilege to define events and phenomena. Feminism represents a challenge to the epistemological privilege of the dominant group. The challenge is to reveal and reduce bias, not to introduce it, as *Booth v. Hvass* claims.

Rather than denoting a single, static interpersonal or interclass relationship, patriarchy refers to multiple structures and relationships that interact with one another. Patriarchy is relevant at each level of the social ecology in ways that engender violence against women and shape responses to it. As feminist theorists have explained, patriarchy includes both ideological and structural components (Dobash and Dobash 1979; Millett 1969; Walby 1990). Both are relevant to violence. Looking at either ideological or structural contributions alone produces a distorted view of the reality of violence (Smith 1990, 1991).

Patriarchy, Gender, and Violence across the Social Ecology

Cultural Factors

Patriarchy is expressed at the cultural level as ideologies about gender, including formal and informal gender norms, that explain and justify patriarchy and its outcomes. Simply because hegemonic gender ideology is male-dominant does not mean that it always takes the form of invidious discrimination. Both "benevolent" and misogynist ideologies about women and men need to be taken into account because both can produce inequality and violence. Even apparently benevolent patriarchal ideologies, such as those positing women's inherent superiority in child care and other forms of reproductive labor, produce significant inequalities that are relevant to the dynamics of violence and abuse.

Likewise, ideologies about men protecting women from other men's violence promote the notion of violence as masculinity-affirming. For example, a man may be expected to punish other men for abusing a woman or girl with whom he has a proprietary relationship (Presser 2003). Historically, another example of "benevolent" sexism, the exclusion of women from jury service, resulted in discrimination against women when cases came to trial. Although the arguments in favor of excusing or excluding women from juries ranged from misogynist references to women's alleged mental inferiority and bias to their putative delicacy, requiring their protection from hearing the ugly details of crimes, the outcome was that women were tried before juries containing only men (Kerber 1998).

Community Factors

Patriarchy is manifested at the community level in such phenomena as the fact that men lead 88 percent of the countries on Earth (Christiansen 2009). For example, 83 percent of the current United States Congress is male, and there has never been a female president of the United States (Center for American Women and Politics 2009). This predominance is relevant to violence against women because politicians write laws and prioritize funding for social services. Structural expressions of male domination fit into this level of the social ecology. Some forms of discrimination against women have been explicitly written into law and enacted through state institutions, such as the historical exemption of marital rape from prosecution (Russell 1982). Others are more informal, such as a police culture that discourages involvement in "domestics" (Buzawa and Buzawa 1996).

Interpersonal Factors

Patriarchy is expressed at the interpersonal level in relationships with family members, intimate partners, and friends. It is expressed in the division of power and work in the home and in men having friends who provide peer support for violence against female partners. For example, women's disproportionate responsibility for child care produces significant and persistent income and resource inequality. Studies in the United States and elsewhere have also found that male batterers use negative assessments of their partners' performance of domestic tasks to justify violence against them, which twists the putative idealization of female caring behavior into a mandate for labor that women are to perform and men are to monitor and evaluate (Anderson and Umberson 2001; Borochowitz 2008; Totten 2003).

Opponents of gender-inclusive understandings of violence claim that women are more likely to use violence against men in the home because of women's alleged equality there. However, the research finds that relationships in which both partners have similar status, such as having a similar education or sharing decision making power in the family, have far lower rates of violence than relationships in which partners have inequitable status (Gelles 1997, 85). Multiple studies investigating the relationship between men's violence against female intimates and power imbalances within couples indicate that inequality is associated with greater violence (Gelles 1997; Moore and Stuart 2005; Yllö 1990). Male-dominant relationships were most closely linked to men's violence against women, female-dominant relationships showed elevated levels of violence, and egalitarian couples had the lowest levels of violence, suggesting that "power imbalance, regardless of which spouse has greater power, may be a critical variable in predicting partner violence" (Moore and Stuart 2005, 55; internal citations omitted).

In addition, Gelles noted that violence is more frequent when there is status incompatibility in a relationship. According to Gelles, status incompatibility, which is distinct from status inequality, "is where the husband, whom society expects to be the head of the family, has less education and a poorer job than his wife" (1997, 85; internal citations omitted). In other words, while patriarchal relationships where men have the highest status are compatible with social norms, relationships in which women have the highest status are incompatible with social norms and are thus at greater risk of violence.

Change over Time (Chronosystem)

Sylvia Walby (1990) has argued that it is necessary to consider the historically specific manifestations of patriarchy and how it changes form over time. Changes over time include such phenomena as the historical context of condoning violence against women or tolerating it within certain limits (Gordon 1988; Kerber 1998; Schneider 2000). In addition to changes in the manifestation of patriarchy throughout history, the chronosystem includes the ways that women's assessments of abusive relationships change over time (Landenburger 1989) as well as how male abusers' explanations of their behavior change over time (Buchbinder and Eisikovits 2004). The cumulative effects of multiple forms of abuse by one person against another over time also fall under the chronosystem, as does the cumulative impact of a life history of multiple victimizations by multiple perpetrators. In other words, the chronosystem is relevant across multiple levels of the social ecology. It shapes individual experiences, the cultural context in which violence acquires meaning, and the interpersonal history of interactions between two people.

Interaction of Multiple Factors (Mesosystem)

Although each individual level of the social ecology is important, the mesosystem is key to understanding violence against intimates because multiple factors at different levels interact with one another. Gender interacts with race, class, age, and other salient social categories in a comprehensive cultural environment. As Frye has explained, the significance of each component of oppression may be unclear when examined individually, but these factors in interaction with one another produce a cumulative "network of forces and barriers which are systematically related and which conspire to the immobilization, reduction and molding of women and the lives we live" (1983, 7). This context makes the gendered dynamics of violence visible. Accordingly, the *Booth* plaintiffs sought to dismantle the approach that considers mesosystem factors in favor of a narrow interpersonal approach to violence.

The research findings on violence and gender indicate that the mesosystem is a critical component to understanding how patriarchal ideology and gendered structural factors interact to contribute to violence in individual relationships. For example, psychological research attempting to measure gender as an individual-level factor that can be identified by asking study participants questions about themselves has failed to find consistent direct correlations between gender and violence. Likewise, research on patriarchy and violence that has attempted to measure patriarchy using individual-level factors such as whether study participants endorse statements about male supremacy has also failed to find consistent direct correlations between patriarchy and violence. Some scholars point to these studies as indications that patriarchal norms are unrelated to male violence and that there is no relationship between patriarchy at the cultural and individual levels (Dutton 2006).

However, research that examines gender in its patriarchal social context has repeatedly found that the interaction of multiple factors explains sex differences in violence and helps to explain why some people are violent and others are not. For example, in their review of psychological research on masculinity and intimate violence, Ted Moore and Gregory Stuart found that "when faced with challenges to their masculine gender role ideology, some men may experience significant conflict or stress and engage in traditionally male behaviors (e.g. violence) to maintain their sense of control and power" (2005, 52; internal citations omitted). Moore and Stuart stated in their review of the research on masculinity and violence,

> The consistent and positive relationship between gender role stress and the use of verbal and physical conflict tactics in relationships suggests that the level of men's appraisal of stress and threat to situations that challenge masculine norms may be a critical component in understanding why some men behave violently. (2005, 52)

This finding links cultural norms for patriarchy to individual-level experiences and behavior. It also mirrors some of the earliest psychological scholarship on violence, which recognized it as disproportionately male, shaped by culture, and masculinity-affirming (Parsons 1947). Jackson Toby conceived the term "compulsive masculinity" as some men's need to demonstrate their masculinity constantly by showing that they do not have any feminine qualities; one such demonstration is the use of violence (1966). According to Toby, the heterosexual nuclear family structure and division of labor explain "why violence, though punishable by law and condemned by custom, nevertheless remains a clandestine masculine ideal in Western culture" (19), especially among marginalized men. Subsequent research has uncovered a more complicated set of relationships between norms producing and inhibiting violence. One important set of studies investigating the interaction of patriarchal gender norms with other social factors is that on patriarchal peer support.

Scholarly Evidence of Patriarchal Peer Support of Violence against Women

Studies have documented the influence of patriarchal peer support for men's violence against women at the mesosystem level in a variety of contexts, including studies of battered wives, dating violence, batterer narratives, campus sexual assault, separation assault, and woman abuse in representative random samples (Bograd 1988; Coleman 1980; DeKeseredy 1996; DeKeseredy and Kelly 1993; DeKeseredy and Schwartz 1998; DeKeseredy and Schwartz 2009; DeKeseredy, Schwartz, Fagan, and Hall 2006; Dobash and Dobash 1979; Gondolf 1988; Gwartney-Gibbs, Stockard, and Bohmer 1987; Schwartz and DeKeseredy 1997; Silverman and Williamson 1997; Smith 1987; Williamson and Silverman 2001). In their study of 109 battered wives, Dobash and Dobash first documented a correlation between high levels of abusive men's socialization with friends and violence against wives (1979). Dobash and Dobash contrasted abusive men's socialization with peers with their wives' social isolation. Abusive men enforced a double standard: they came and went as they pleased yet intensely monitored their wives' interactions with others. Characteristic of this imbalance was the expectation that women be always at home ready to cater to their husbands and the husbands' interpretation of the failure to meet demands for service from women as attacks against men's rights as head of household.

Lee Bowker (1986) also stressed the importance of male peer support for violence against wives in his study of one thousand battered women.

Bowker found "the more frequently a man socialized with his friends, the more severely and extensively he battered his wife" (102). Accordingly, Bowker recommended that the influence of male peers who are supportive of violence against women should be addressed in treatment for male batterers. Bowker hypothesized that involvement with male peers reinforced batterers' ideas about entitlement to "standards of gratification demanding domestic dominance" (103) and observed, "There is no national lobby favoring wife-beating. However, the many male friends and acquaintances who support patriarchal dominance of the family and the use of violence to enforce it may amount to what we might call a masculine culture of violence" (103).

Like the psychological studies Moore and Stuart reviewed, more recent research has empirically studied patriarchal peer support for violence against women as a contributing factor to violence. Michael Smith tested feminist theories about patriarchal ideology and male peer support for woman abuse in his study of 604 Toronto women (1987; 1990; 1991). Using a mixed-method approach that supplemented items from the CTS with additional quantitative and qualitative items, Smith combined factors from across the social ecology to measure the relationship of patriarchy to violence. He found that patriarchal beliefs and the approval of violence against women were positively related to woman abuse and that men with lower socioeconomic status were more likely to endorse patriarchal beliefs and more likely to have used violence against their partners (1990). This finding suggests that patriarchy at the individual level interacts with cultural-level expectations about masculinity to contribute to violence at the interpersonal level.

Smith asked the respondents in his study if they thought their husband's friends would approve of a husband slapping his wife in a variety of situations. He found that "husbands with male friends who would, in the eyes of the respondents, approve of a husband slapping his wife were significantly more likely than were husbands without such friends to have physically abused their wives at least once during the marriage" (Smith 1991, 514).

Most recently, DeKeseredy and Schwartz (DeKeseredy and Schwartz 2009; DeKeseredy et al. 2006; Godenzi, Schwartz, and DeKeseredy 2001; Schwartz and DeKeseredy 1997) and Silverman and Williamson (Silverman and Williamson 1997; Williamson and Silverman 2001) have developed and empirically tested what they term patriarchal peer support theory. DeKeseredy and Schwartz's model of patriarchal peer support describes "the multidimensional attachments men form to male peers" who abuse female intimate partners or "provide resources that perpetuate and legitimate such assaults." Patriarchal peer support theory stresses the mesosystem, especially the interaction of individual, interpersonal, and cultural factors (DeKeseredy et al. 2006). DeKeseredy and Schwartz (1998) relate male peer-group support for violence against women to "rape culture," the culture normalizing male dominance and the objectification of women in more or less hostile forms (Brownmiller 1975; Buchwald 1993). This approach, like that of Dobash and Dobash, not only emphasizes the impossibility of understanding any single aspect of violence and abuse out of context; it stresses the dialogical relationship between multiple factors.

Patriarchal peer support theory underscores conflicts that emerge at the intersection of patriarchal social expectations and the realities of interpersonal relationships (DeKeseredy et al. 2006). Men are "regularly exposed to messages from other men suggesting that a real man is not under the control of a woman; a real man . . . does not accept attacks on his masculine authority" (Schwartz and DeKeseredy 1997). The emphasis on the interaction between social and familial patriarchy in *creating* relationship stress is one area where patriarchal peer support theory improves upon other theories of violence, which tend to decontextualize and individualize stress. The interaction between expectations for interpersonal relationships and cultural male supremacy helps to explain how even "benevolent" sexism can coexist with attitudes condoning men's prerogative to discipline, violently or otherwise, women with whom they have a proprietary relationship. For example, men who grow up in patriarchal homes may be more likely to normalize gender inequality, especially if their fathers abused their mothers (DeKeseredy et al. 2006; Williamson and Silverman 2001). It is in this context that simple arguments with female intimates rise to the status of threats to men's identity and justify physical attacks that men label as defensive and reciprocal to women's provocation.

Gail Williamson and Jay Silverman (2001) summarized the research suggesting that peer influence moderates other contributing factors to violence, such as witnessing or experiencing violence in the home. Williamson and Silverman argued that the interaction between peer support for violence against women and other variables may help to explain why some people who witness abuse as children go on to perpetrate it but many others do not. The peer association factor may also help to explain sex differences in the correlation between witnessing and perpetration or victimization. Williamson and Silverman also found that "associating with peers who advocate and perpetrate dating violence was related to abusing one's own female partners" (2001, 543–44).

Deborah Reitzel-Jaffe and David Wolfe's study of 585 male college students (2001) found that

> violence in men's family of origin predicted abuse in their own dating relationships and predicted the development of negative beliefs about gender and interpersonal violence. These negative beliefs in turn predicted their own use of violence or coercion in relationships and their association with peers who endorse violent attitudes and behavior. Finally, the association with negative peers also predicted the occurrence of abuse toward a dating partner. (2001, 108–9)[2]

Reitzel-Jaffe and Wolfe's statistical analysis found that one of the strongest paths in their model was "the relationship between participants' negative beliefs and the abusive behaviors of their best friends" and noted, "The relationship from negative peer associations to participants' experiences with relationship abuse was also significant and strong" (109). Their findings suggest that men with attitudes supportive of violence against women seek out peers with similar beliefs and that these peer associations are in turn associated with the perpetration of abuse.

Although some commentators assume that the most important message Western men receive about violence against women is the unequivocal command "never hit a girl" (Brott 1994), the research finds that women and men receive and subscribe to a more complicated set of mixed messages about violence that often mitigate or suspend the admonition against violence against women (DeKeseredy and Kelly 1993; Howe 1997; McCarthy 1994–95; Wood 2001). While many men, including those convicted of violent crimes, endorse the idea that men should never "hit a girl," they can also easily enumerate the transgressions that release them from that prohibition. According to this logic, men preserve the prerogative to use violence against women, to define what counts as violence, to decide how women should behave, and to decide which women deserve chivalrous "protection" and under what circumstances.

The "no hitting girls" rule is also instructive for what it implies—that it is acceptable for men to use violence against other men. As every study of human violence has documented, men's greatest risk is from other men. The expectation that men know how to use violence and have the capacity to produce violence on demand in certain social circumstances is one area where gendered socialization is highly visible. Men who "hit like girls" or "fight like women" are objects of derision. Women who use violence are violating the social norms for femininity, and their sexuality may be called into question. Also, many men who abuse women call them lesbians. As Pharr points out, this gendered, sexualized slur contains the implicit threat that a woman can be cast out of the "protection" offered by patriarchal, heterosexual relationships and thus established as fair game and a legitimate target for further violence and abuse.

Critics of gender-inclusive violence research claim that what they term feminist theories cannot account for why the majority of men do not use violence against female intimates. They also claim that theories that take gender into consideration cannot accommodate women's use of violence or male victims. However, these arguments reveal a fundamental failure to comprehend the extant research, which stresses the interaction of ideological and structural factors at the mesosystem level and pays attention to sex, gender, and patriarchy. Indeed, gender-blind explanations for violence against intimates consistently fail to explain why human violence, including violence against intimates, is so profoundly, persistently, and disproportionately perpetrated by men. Simply ignoring gendered forms of violence and the research documenting sex differences in violence does not solve this problem. As this review of the literature relevant to violence, gender, and patriarchy makes clear, patriarchy may be described as "unitary" only insofar as the different manifestations of patriarchy relate to one another across the entire system of the social ecology. Patriarchy is relevant to understanding violence and its effects at each level of the social ecology

Antifeminists who ask why services and scholars focus on men's violence against women might themselves be asked why they ignore men's greatest risk of violence—that from other men—and instead focus on the tiny portion of violence men experience from women. Advocates for men's safety might be expected to emphasize the greatest harms to men, such as armed conflict, and men's violence against acquaintances and strangers rather than the portion of violence that presents the smallest risk to them.

7 | Conclusion

Booth v. Hvass endeavored to eliminate services for battered women and other victims of domestic abuse by arguing that women and men are similarly situated with regard to domestic violence. In posing an equal protection claim, *Booth v. Hvass* sought to undermine feminism itself and prompt a return to earlier understandings of violence that held victims responsible and enabled abusers to evade responsibility for their actions and to maintain control of their victims. The lawsuit also explicitly sought to obliterate feminist scholarship that takes gender into account and to start again with men's experiences at the center. However, juxtaposing *Booth v. Hvass* with batterer narratives and antifeminist commentaries in popular media and scholarship reveals exactly what is at stake in this approach to violence against intimates.

Inspection of claims about violence against intimates as gender-free reveals that such assertions are often based on the conflation of the concepts of sex and gender. Statements about the gender neutrality of violence against intimates also frequently imply that the occurrence of perpetration and victimization in both sexes means that the violence is equivalent and not shaped in any way by gendered socialization. Thus claims about the equivalency of violence against intimates across sex differences tend to dismiss or ignore the well-documented gendered outcomes, demographics, and dynamics of violence. Claims that violence is gender-free focus on factors at the individual and interpersonal levels of the social ecology to the exclusion of other the other levels and attempt to focus attention narrowly on incident-based intervention rather than prevention.

The denial that violence against intimates is gendered and sex-asymmetrical is, at best, a demonstration of inadequate understandings of the extant research on gender and violence and, at worst, an intentional attack on feminism and its influence that regards the elimination of laws and services assisting battered women and other victims of abuse as acceptable collateral damage, or even the desired outcome. In addition to explicit claims about undermining feminism, antagonism toward feminist and other gender-inclusive research is evident in efforts to de-emphasize the adverse effects of men's victimization of women, to divert attention away from male offenders and the social construction of patri-archal masculinity, and to collapse the very different dynamics of vio-lence as women and men experience it. The antifeminist agenda is most explicit in the *Booth* plaintiffs' attempt to eliminate services to all victims of battering rather than acknowledging the sexed and gendered nature of the violence. As a result of ignorance or ideology, proponents of gender-blind perspectives hinder the dissemination of accurate information about violence and pose a threat to existing services for all victims.

By juxtaposing discourses on violence that are normally considered separately and in isolation, the commonalities and differences between batterer accounts and other discourses on violence and abuse become clear. Such comparisons allow the opportunity to understand better im-plicit, conflicting, and taken-for-granted cultural norms and values around violence and gender. Comparing multiple discourses on violence against intimates reveals the "truth effects" hidden within different con-ceptualizations of it (Foucault 1972). The *Booth* lawsuit and other anti-feminist discourses typify violence in many ways similar to how men who batter women minimize, deny, excuse, and justify their violence. Anti-feminist discourses also attempt to trivialize the experiences of battered women by asserting that men are harmed by violence at rates similar to women, and that men's victimization is exacerbated by approaches to violence that acknowledge gender and patriarchy. Drawing out the con-nection between batterer narratives on the one hand and the *Booth* case on the other reveals how influential media and legal discourses actually support batterers in the ways of thinking that contribute to their con-tinued use of violence. The prevalence of narratives that fail to confront male batterers' beliefs about violence against women decisively functions as a form of patriarchal peer support for woman abuse at the cultural level.

Positioning the *Booth v. Hvass* sex-symmetry claim alongside the re-search on sex differences in violence, the salience of gender and patri-archy to violence, antifeminist discourses, and batterer narratives also clarifies how those who know the most about violence against women, including batterers, refer frequently to patriarchal gender norms to explain men's violence against women. Given that even batterers implicate gender as an important factor in their violence, and given the breadth and depth of feminist and other research that accounts for gender, *Booth*'s demand for gender-blindness is impossible to sustain. Gender-blindness is not gender neutrality. Discourses about violence against intimates that fail to account for gender reinscribe the centrality of men's experiences and subvert those of battered women.

The *Booth* plaintiffs' claim that domestic violence is sex-symmetrical was unsupported even by the research they submitted in defense of their complaint. Instead, the research and the misleading ways in which it is sometimes used serve to underscore the necessity for researchers to be clear about the type of violence under investigation. In order to be useful, writing on violence must be specific and explicit. Scholars' recommendations for services and policies should also be relevant to the kind of violence studied. Schwartz asked, "What is the entire point of studying violence against women?" (2002, 819). If the point is to understand violence better, scholars need to work to recontextualize violence and the research on it. If the goal is to decrease violence against women, we need to interrupt the ways of talking about it and understanding it that implicitly enable it to continue.

Learning to recognize the echoes of batterer narratives in other discourses can be a valuable tool in efforts to decrease violence. Regardless of the intentions behind it, rhetoric that parrots abusers and blames victims by proclaiming sex symmetry in violence serves to reproduce the conditions that enable it. The similarity between batterers' accounts of their behavior and the arguments presented in *Booth v. Hvass* illustrates what is at stake in this debate. The *Booth* case illustrates the political nature of discourse and the ways that discourses can be used to contain ways of thinking and speaking that challenge hegemonic understandings of social issues. In order to move forward in understanding violence, we cannot distort its dynamics by conflating dissimilar phenomena. We need to make our thinking about violence more nuanced by expanding the number of factors that we take into account, not by artificially limiting our perspective.

Multidimensional ecological models provide useful tools for understanding the complex and multifaceted etiology of violence against women and men. As we expand the scope of violence research to include more factors, we need to maintain the complexity of these models instead of collapsing all violence into an amorphous body. One-size fits-all responses have never been adequate for preventing and responding to violence against women, and they are similarly inappropriate for dealing with other kinds of violence.

Directions for Future Research

This book explores some connections between discourses on violence in multiple contexts. It provides a synthesis of the extant research with media and legal accounts of intimate violence. As a case study, it has several limitations. This book looks in detail at one particular case, but no one legal case is representative of all contemporary discourses on violence. The book used some of the most conservative sources on sex differences in violence and abuse and drew heavily from official sources. Accordingly, it duplicates the weaknesses of these sources, including underreporting and sampling biases. The section on patriarchy and violence only scratches the surface of the research on violence and masculinities. Contemporary research on masculinities stresses the ways that gender is performed in multiple ways in different contexts. Given the nature of legal and media battles, I have chosen to focus on establishing that patriarchal gender contributes to violence rather than reviewing the ways in which multiple varieties of masculinity shape crime. Finally, because the book is a synthesis of published sources rather than an original study, it does not provide a new test of the connections between patriarchy and violence. Instead it seeks to articulate and explore how these connections play out in one case.

Future research has the potential to increase our understanding of violence and abuse in its many forms and contexts. Scholars have already begun the process of conducting careful empirical research on the dynamics of violence in multiple populations. Research on the many facets of gendered violence is becoming increasingly interdisciplinary, and scholars can benefit from integrating the multiple literatures on violence. Scholars of violence need to pay attention to the political, legal, and cultural contexts in which efforts to end violence play out. In addition, advocates and scholars need to continue to work together in order to ensure that the research produced reflects real people's experiences and produces useable data that can address their needs.

More research is needed on the less common forms of violence against intimates, including same-sex violence and women's violence. Scholars who want to study women's use of violence should familiarize themselves with the growing literature in this area, much of which has been conducted by feminist scholars and has investigated contributing factors at all levels of the social ecology. Despite the difficulties associated with small sample sizes, we also need information about violence against transgendered people as well as against people who identify as bisexual. What does violence and abuse against intimates look like in these contexts? What services are currently available, and what others are needed? Removing gendered pronouns is not adequate to the task of building empirically based understandings of the unique dynamics of violence in these different contexts. We need to work to articulate and test theories of violence that can account for contributing factors at all levels of the social ecology for each of these contexts. We need to talk to both survivors and perpetrators of violence.

There is also a need for more research that teases out the impact of the intersecting oppressions of sexism, racism, classism, and immigrant status. Although antifeminist fathers' rights groups like those involved in the *Booth* case are almost exclusively populated by white heterosexual men, there are some similarities between the push for gender-blindness and color-blindness. Research on the promotion of color-blind and gender-blind language as a response to anti-oppression work has the potential to inform efforts to address racism, sexism, and heterosexism in policy and practice.

Finally, it is important to study the connections between marginal and mainstream manifestations of antifeminist backlash. Where and how do efforts to reassert patriarchy affect abused women the most? As the proliferation of antifeminist father's groups indicates, family law is a central location of struggle for abused women and especially abused mothers. Criminologists and other scholars who study violence need to broaden their gaze to include the family law system in addition to criminal and civil law. Many more abused women will come into contact with the family law system than will report abuse to the police. Popular cultural conversations about families continue to constitute an essential context for understanding violence against intimates.

Policy Recommendations

Policy recommendations for addressing woman abuse and other forms of violence share common ground with critical approaches to other social problems. Scholars widely recognize that efforts to decrease social inequality and provide sustainable options for economic support, housing, transportation, health care, education, and community resources are key to ameliorating violence as well as many other social problems. The gendered nature of woman abuse requires that policy efforts in these areas recognize the gendered aspects of these putatively generic concerns. For example, women's disproportionate responsibility for raising children means that affordable child care is essential to maintaining employment. Women's lower wages mean that their ability to leave abusive relationships is shaped by persistent income inequality. In addition to crafting resources that ameliorate gendered inequalities in order to allow abused women to escape from their abusers, we need to address the common contributing factors to violence and patriarchy.

Finally, it is important to recognize that the fierce resistance to efforts to understand violence as a complex and gendered form of human behavior is a sign of the successes of the battered women's movement and the feminist movement. The vitriolic tone of the *Booth* complaint and other attacks against services for battered women show how threatening change is to some. While out of touch with reality, the *Booth* plaintiffs' perception of male persecution in the context of a feminist-controlled state indicates that some men are profoundly threatened by the prospect of state responses to violence against women. Antifeminist attacks not only attempt to undermine the changes that have already been made; they also provide teachable moments by revealing hegemonic social norms and values that are so taken for granted as to be invisible. Ironically, the insistence that feminism is wrongheaded or unnecessary underscores the lingering opposition to women's equality. Attacks against the services and policies that assist abused women indicate that we need to pay more attention to the interrelationship between patriarchy and woman abuse. As a result, feminism and its insights continue to be absolutely essential to future work to end violence.

Notes

Introduction

1. The plaintiffs included Scott Booth, Thomas D. Loyd, Frank Solchaga, David Witte, Scott Wyman, Charles Perrin, Warren Higgins, Knute Gladen, Michael Seeber, Terry Nyblom, and Stephen Blake, collectively identified as representing the R-KIDS Legal Action Committee; Richard Doyle, identified as representing the Men's Defense Association; and William J. Hageman, Charles H. Hurd, Kyle Knutson, Jim Lovestar, Yves Nadeau, and Pradeep Ramanathan, identified as representing the National Coalition of Free Men, Twin Cities Chapter. One of the men, Warren Higgins, is named in the original lawsuit but not the appeal. John Remington Graham and Mark A. Olson represented the plaintiffs. The defendants were Sheryl Ramstad Hvass, Commissioner of Corrections; Michael O'Keefe, Commissioner of Human Services; Charles R. Weaver, Commissioner of Public Safety; and Christine Jax, Commissioner of Children, Families, and Learning for the state of Minnesota. The defense was represented by Mark B. Levinger and Jennifer Park, Assistant Attorneys General. Defendant-intervenors on the initial case included the Domestic Abuse Project, the Central Minnesota Task Force on Battered Women, and the Lakes Crisis Center, organizations that received funding through Minnesota's domestic abuse statutes and provided emergency services for female and male survivors of abuse. Beverly Balos and Maury Landsman represented the defendant-intervenors with assistance from law students Karen Terese Olsen and Erica Weston. On appeal, *amici curiae* included the Minnesota Coalition for Battered Women and the Domestic Violence Legislative Alliance, represented by Loretta M. Frederick.

2. R-KIDS stands for Remembering Kids in Divorce Settlements. Its website is http://www.rkids.org/. The Men's Defense Association website is http://www.mensdefense.org/. The National Coalition of Free Men (NCFM) changed its name to the National Coalition for Men in 2008. NCFM's Twin Cities website is http://www.ncfm.org/chapters/tc/. The national organization is accessible through links on the site.

3. There is in fact no one law called the Minnesota Battered Women's Act. The Minnesota statues cited by the plaintiffs (section 611A.31 through 611A.36) are a series of statues that provide a mechanism for disbursing state and federal funding for services for battered women and other victims of domestic abuse. In 2000, this set of the Minnesota statutes was titled "Battered Women and Domestic Abuse." The statutes have since been revised and the section is now titled, "Crime Victims: Rights, Programs, Agencies."

4. Equal protection is a legal term referencing part of the Fourteenth Amendment, the equal protection clause, of the United States Constitution. The relevant section reads, "No state shall make or enforce any law which shall abridge the privileges or immunities of citizens of the United States; nor shall any state deprive any person of life, liberty, or property, without due process of law; nor deny to any person within its jurisdiction the Equal Protection of the laws."

5. The battered women's movement refers to grassroots efforts beginning in the 1970s to establish assistance for abused women and their children. The battered women's movement is an umbrella term for organizing by such groups as shelters, state coalitions, and women's organizations. The movement focused on establishing essential services for survivors, implementing legal reform, and promoting social change to end violence against women. See Schechter (1982) for an in-depth history of the movement in the United States.

Chapter 2. *Booth v. Hvass*

1. The plaintiffs did not provide evidence that any man had been denied services in Minnesota in any of their case documents and affirmed that they had not sought services. In fact, published notes from an R-KIDS meeting that took place in 1999 when the case was being prepared noted that "Swift County (Benson) Minnesota (female) employees responded with consideration and kindness to three battered men who sought help, according to R-Kids member Frank Solchaga. Usually, abused and battered men are ignored and sent away without any assistance from social workers" (R-KIDS 1999).

2. See, for example, *Nollet v. Justices of the Trial Court of the Commonwealth of Massachusetts* (2000), *Blumhorst v. Jewish Family Services* (2005), and *Woods v. Horton* (aka *Woods v. Shewry*) (2008).

3. See Dragiewicz and Lindgren 2009 for an in-depth discussion of the *Woods* case and the situation in California. California is in a unique legal position because it uses a strict standard of scrutiny for gender classification. Other states use the strict standard of scrutiny for race but an intermediate standard for gender.

4. In fact, the only place Minnesota's domestic violence legislation does distinguish between women and men is in the provision of funding for freestanding

shelters for battered women and their children. All other aspects of the legislation are sex- and gender-neutral.

5. Domestic violence shelters usually house men in hotels rather than in shared bedrooms with women at purpose built domestic violence shelters.

6. Race and gender are suspect classification categories, but the government allows discrimination against groups to whom the protected category status does not apply, for example lesbian women and gay men.

7. The legal writing uses the terms "gender" and "sex" interchangeably.

8. Saunders has since been promoted to full professor and continues to publish in the field of violence and abuse.

9. Saunders later published a version of these arguments as the article, "Are Physical Assaults by Wives and Girlfriends a Major Social Problem? A Review of the Literature" in a 2002 issue of *Violence Against Women* 8, 12:1424–48.

Chapter 3. Popular Discourses

1. The O. J. Simpson and Lorena Bobbitt and John Bobbitt cases have received the most media attention. See Kozol 1995 and McCarthy 1994-95 for discussion of these cases.

2. For example see Berk et al. 1993; Breines and Gordon 1983; Davis 1987; De-Keseredy 1992; Dobash et al. 1992; Osthoff 2002; and Schwartz and DeKeseredy 1993.

Chapter 4. Batterer Narratives

1. The CTS is a quantitative measurement tool that has been frequently utilized and critiqued. For a detailed description of the CTS, see Straus, Gelles, and Steinmetz 1981. For an in-depth discussion of critiques of the CTS, see De-Keseredy and Schwartz 1998b and Kimmel 2002.

2. Cavanagh et al. studied men who had been convicted of at least one violent crime against their partners, but they noted that many of the men had also been previously charged. The researchers also interviewed the partners of the men.

Chapter 5. Sex Differences

1. See for example Archer 2000a, b; Bograd 1990b; Berliner 1990; Frieze 2000; Kurz 1993; McNeely and Mann 1990; McNeely and Robinson-Simpson 1987, 1988; O'Leary 2000; Saunders 1986, 1988; Straus 1993; and White et al. 2000. The journal *Violence Against Women* ran a three-volume special issue on women's use of

violence from November 2002 through January 2003. These special issues may be seen in part as a response to often-repeated claims about sex symmetry in domestic violence. Many of the articles in the collection address these claims specifically. The research presented therein moves well beyond arguments about the numbers of women and men who admit to using violence in order to investigate the patterns and dynamics of women's and men's violence.

The National Institutes of Justice also convened a "Gender Symmetry Workshop" on the measurement of violence on November 20, 2000, in Arlington, Virginia. The resulting papers were published as a special issue of *Violence Against Women*. See Rosen 2006.

2. See for example DeKeseredy 1994, 1996; DeKeseredy and Kelly 1993; Fekete 1994; Fox 1993; Gartner 1993; and Kelly 1994. Also see H. Johnson 1995, 1996.

3. Critiques of the CTS, similar measures, and the claims made using the findings have been published repeatedly since 1977. For a review of these critiques, see DeKeseredy and Schwartz 1998 and Kimmel 2002.

4. Additional detailed information about homicides is collected through fatality review processes at the local level. See for example Fawcett et al. 2008.

5. For reviews of the homicide literature see Barnard et al. 1982; Campbell et al. 2007; Garcia, Soria, and Hurwitz 2007; Kellermann and Mercy 1992; Websdale 1999; and Wilson and Daly 1992.

6. The numbers of men were too small to be statistically established and thus were estimated.

Chapter 6. Gender and Patriarchy

1. *Tough Guise: Violence, Media and the Crisis in Masculinity* is a documentary about the ways that film and television representations of masculinity have become increasingly violent over time.

2. Reitzel-Jaffe and Wolfe defined negative beliefs as negative attitudes toward women, acceptance of interpersonal violence, rape myth acceptance, and adversarial sexual beliefs.

References

Adams, D. 1989. Identifying the assaultive husband in court: You be the judge. *Boston Bar Journal* July/August, 33–34.

Amended complaint. 2000. *Booth v. Hvass*, 302 F.3d 849 (8th Cir. 2002).

American Medical Association. 2000. Women's health: Sex- and gender-based differences in health and disease. http://www.ama-assn.org/ama/no-index/about-ama/13607.shtml.

Anderson, K. L., and D. Umberson. 2001. Gendering violence: Masculinity and power in men's accounts of domestic violence. *Gender and Society* 15, 3: 358–80.

Appellants' reply to amici curiae. 2001. *Booth v. Hvass*, 302 F.3d 849 (8th Cir. 2002).

Archer, J. 2000a. Sex differences in aggression between heterosexual partners: A meta-analytic review. *Psychological Bulletin* 126, 5: 651–80.

Archer, J. 2000b. Sex differences in physical aggression to partners: A reply to Frieze (2000), O'Leary (2000), and White, Smith, Koss, and Figueredo (2000). *Psychological Bulletin* 126, 5: 697–702.

Arias, I. and S. R. H. Beach. 1987. Validity of self-reports of marital violence. *Journal of Family Violence* 2, 2: 139–49.

Armstrong, L., and L. Tennenhouse. 1989. Introduction: Representing violence, or 'how the west was won.' In *The violence of representation: Literature and the history of violence*, ed. L. Armstrong and L. Tennenhouse, 1–28. New York: Routledge.

Bachman, R., and L. E. Saltzman. 1995. *Violence against women: Estimates from the redesigned survey*. Washington, DC: US Department of Justice, Office of Justice Programs, Bureau of Justice Statistics.

Balos, B., M. Landsman, K. T. Olson, and E. Weston. 2001. Appellee intervenors' brief for *Booth v. Hvass*, 302 F.3d 849 (8th Cir. 2002).

Bancroft, L. 2002. *Why does he do that? Inside the minds of angry and controlling men*. New York: Berkley Books.

Barnard, G. W., H. Vera, M. I. Vera, and G. Newman. 1982. Till death do us part: A study of spouse murder. *Bulletin of the American Academy of Psychiatry and the Law* 10, 4: 271–80.

Barnett, M. 2001. Affidavit for *Booth v. Hvass*, 302 F.3d 849 (8th Cir. 2002).

Berliner, L. 1990. Domestic violence: A humanist or feminist issue? *Journal of Interpersonal Violence* 5, 1:128–35.

Berns, N. 2001. Degendering the problem and gendering the blame: Political discourse on women and violence. *Gender and Society* 15, 2: 262–81.

Berns, N. 2004. *Framing the victim: Domestic violence, media and social problems.* Hawthorne, NY: Aldine de Gruyter.

Bible, A., S. D. Dasgupta, and S. Osthoff. 2002. Guest editors' introduction. *Violence Against Women* 8, 11: 1267–70.

Bibus, M. 2001. Affidavit for *Booth v. Hvass*, 302 F.3d 849 (8th Cir. 2002).

Biroscak, B. J., P. K. Smith, and L. A. Post. 2006. A practical approach to public health surveillance of violent deaths related to intimate partner relationships. *Public Health Reports* 121, 4: 393–99.

Blumhorst v. Jewish Family Services of Los Angeles, 126 Cal. App. 4th 993, 24 Cal. Rptr. 3d 474, (2005).

Bograd, M. 1988. How battered women and abusive men account for domestic violence: Excuses, justifications, or explanations? In *Coping with family violence: Research and policy perspectives*, ed. G.T. Hotaling, D. Finkelhor, J. T. Kirkpatrick, and M. A. Straus, 60–77. Newbury Park, CA: Sage.

Bograd, M. 1990a. Feminist perspectives on wife abuse: An introduction. In *Feminist perspectives on wife abuse*, ed. K. Yllö and M. Bograd, 11–26. Newbury Park CA: Sage.

Bograd, M. 1990b. Why we need gender to understand human violence. *Journal of Interpersonal Violence* 5: 132–35.

Booth v. Hvass, 302 F.3d 849 (8th Cir. 2002), *cert. denied*, 537 U.S. 1108 (2003).

Borochowitz, D. Y. 2008. The taming of the shrew: Batterers' constructions of their wives' narratives. *Violence Against Women* 14, 10: 1166–80.

Bowker, L. H. 1986. *Ending the violence: A guidebook based on the experience of 1,000 battered wives.* Holmes Beach, FL: Learning Publications.

Bowker, L. H., ed. 1998. *Masculinities and violence.* Thousand Oaks, CA: Sage.

Boyd, S. B. 2003. *Child custody, law, and women's work.* Toronto, ON: Oxford University Press.

Breines, W. and L. Gordon. 1983. The new scholarship on family violence. *Signs* 8, 3: 490–531.

Bronfenbrenner, U. 1979. *The Ecology of human development: Experiments by nature and design.* Cambridge, MA: Harvard University Press.

Bronfenbrenner, U. 1986. Ecology of the family as a context for human development: Research perspectives. *Developmental Psychology* 22: 723–42.

Brooks, R. 1997. Feminists negotiate the legislative branch: The Violence Against Women Act. In *Feminists negotiate the state: The politics of domestic violence*, ed. C. R. Daniels, 65–82. Lanham, MD: University Press of America.

Brott, A. 1994. Battered men: The full story. Fathersgettheshaft.com, http://river .yodns.com/~socmen/archive/battered_men.htm.

Browne, A., and K. R. Williams. 1993. Gender, intimacy and lethal violence: Trends from 1976 through 1987. *Gender and Society* 7, 1: 78–98.

Brownmiller, S. 1975. *Against our will: Men, women and rape.* New York: Bantam Books.

Buchbinder, E., and Z. Eisikovits. 2004. Between normality and deviance: The breakdown of batterers' identity following police intervention. *Journal of Interpersonal Violence* 19, 4: 443–67.

Buchwald, E., P. Fletcher, and M. Roth, eds. 1993. *Transforming a rape culture.* Minneapolis, MN: Milkweed Editions.

Bureau of Justice Statistics. 2007. *Statistics about crime and victims: Victim characteristics.* Bureau of Justice Statistics, http://web.archive.org/web/ 20080716060658/http://www.ojp.usdoj.gov/bjs/cvict_v.htm.

Buzawa, E. S., and C. G. Buzawa. 1996. *Domestic violence: The criminal justice response.* 2nd ed. Thousand Oaks, CA: Sage.

Campbell, J. C., N. Glass, P. W. Sharps, K. Laughon, and T. Bloom. 2007. Intimate partner homicide: Review and implications of research and policy. *Trauma, Violence and Abuse* 8, 3: 246–69.

Carlson, B. E. 1984. Causes and maintenance of domestic violence: An ecological analysis. *Social Services Review* 58, 4: 569–87.

Catalano, S. 2007. *Intimate partner violence in the United States.* Washington, DC: Bureau of Justice Statistics.

Catlett, B. S., and J. E. Artis. 2004. Critiquing the case for marriage promotion: How the promarriage movement misrepresents domestic violence research. *Violence Against Women* 10, 11: 1226–44.

Cavanagh, K., R. E. Dobash, R. P. Dobash, and R. Lewis. 2001. 'Remedial work': Men's strategic responses to their violence against intimate female partners. *Sociology* 35, 3: 695–714.

Center for American Women and Politics. 2009. Women in elective office. Center for American Women and Politics, http://www.cawp.rutgers.edu.

Cerulo, K. A. 1998. *Deciphering violence: The cognitive structure of right and wrong.* New York: Routledge.

Chesler, P. 1994. *Patriarchy: Notes of an expert witness.* Monroe, ME: Common Courage Press.

Christiansen, M. K. I. 2009. Worldwide guide to women in leadership, http:// www.guide2womenleaders.com.

Chunn, D. E., S. B. Boyd, and H. Lessard, eds. 2007. *Reaction and resistance: Feminism, law, and social change.* Vancouver: University of British Columbia Press.

Coleman, K. 1980. Conjugal violence: What 33 men report. *Journal of Marital and Family Therapy* 6, 2: 207–13.

Collier, R., and S. Sheldon. 2006. Fathers' rights, fatherhood and law reform: International perspectives. In *Fathers' rights activism and law reform in comparative perspective*, ed. R. Collier and S. Sheldon, 1–26. Portland, OR: Hart.

Condit, C. M. 1989. The rhetorical limits of polysemy. *Critical Studies in Mass Communication* 6, 2: 103–22.

Connell, R. W. 2000. *The men and the boys*. Berkeley and Los Angeles: University of California Press.

Connell, R. W. 2002. On hegemonic masculinity and violence: Response to Jefferson and Hall. *Theoretical Criminology* 6, 1: 89–99.

Connell, R. W., and J. W. Messerschmidt. 2005. Hegemonic masculinity: Rethinking the concept. *Gender and Society* 19, 6: 829–59.

Consalvo, M. 1998a. '3 Shot dead in courthouse': Examining news coverage of domestic violence and mail-order brides. *Women's Studies in Communication* 21, 2: 188–211.

Consalvo, M. 1998b. Hegemony, domestic violence, and 'Cops': A critique of concordance. *Journal of Popular Film and Television* 26, 2: 62–70.

Cook, P. W. 1997. Abused men: The hidden side of domestic violence. Westport, CT: Praeger.

Craig v. Boren, 429 U.S. 190 (1976).

Crowley, J. E. 2009. Fathers' rights groups, domestic violence and political countermobilization. *Social Forces* 88, 2: 723–56.

Dakota County Attorney's Office. 2000. *Confronting domestic violence*. Hastings, MN: Dakota County Attorney's Office.

Daly, M., and M. Wilson. 1988. *Homicide*. Hawthorne, NY: Aldine de Gruyter.

Dasgupta, S. D. 2002. A framework for understanding women's use of nonlethal violence in intimate heterosexual relationships. *Violence Against Women* 8, 11: 1364–89.

Davis, A. 2000. The color of violence against women. Colorlines: News for Action, http://www.colorlines.com/article.php?ID=72.

DeKeseredy, W. S. 1994. Addressing the complexities of woman abuse in dating: A response to Gartner and Fox. *Canadian Journal of Sociology* 19, 1: 75–80.

DeKeseredy, W. S. 1996. The Canadian National Survey on woman abuse in university/college dating relationships: Biofeminist panic transmission or critical inquiry? *Canadian Journal of Criminology* 38, 1: 81–104.

DeKeseredy, W. S. 1999. Tactics of the antifeminist backlash against Canadian national woman abuse surveys. *Violence Against Women* 5, 11: 1258–76.

DeKeseredy, W. S. 2000. Current controversies on defining non-lethal violence against women in intimate heterosexual relationships: Empirical implications. *Violence Against Women* 6, 7: 728-46.

DeKeseredy, W. S., and M. Dragiewicz. 2007. Understanding the complexities of feminist perspectives on woman abuse: A commentary on Donald G.

Dutton's *Rethinking domestic violence. Violence Against Women* 13, 8: 874–84.

DeKeseredy, W. S., and K. Kelly. 1993. Woman abuse in university and college dating relationships: The contribution of ideology and familial patriarchy. *The Journal of Human Justice* 4: 25–52.

DeKeseredy, W. S., M. Rogness, and M. D. Schwartz. 2004. Separation/divorce sexual assault: The current state of social scientific knowledge. *Aggression and Violent Behavior* 9: 675–91.

DeKeseredy, W. S., and M. D. Schwartz. 1998a. *Woman abuse on campus: Results from the Canadian National Survey.* Thousand Oaks, CA: Sage.

DeKeseredy, W. S., and M. D. Schwartz. 1998b. Measuring the extent of woman abuse in intimate heterosexual relationships: A critique of the Conflict Tactics Scales. National Online Resource Center on Violence Against Women, http://new.vawnet.org/Assoc_Files_VAWnet/AR_ctscrit.pdf.

DeKeseredy, W.S., and M. D. Schwartz. 2009. *Dangerous exits: Escaping abusive relationships in rural America.* New Brunswick, NJ: Rutgers University Press.

DeKeseredy, W.S., M. D. Schwartz, D. Fagen, and M. Hall. 2006. Separation/divorce sexual assault: The contribution of male support. *Feminist Criminology* 1, 3: 228–50.

Dobash, R. E., and R. P. Dobash. 1979. *Violence against wives: A case against the patriarchy.* New York: Free Press.

Dobash, R. E., and R. P. Dobash. 1992. *Women, violence and social change.* London: Routledge.

Dobash, R. E., and R. P. Dobash. 1998. Cross-border encounters: Challenges and opportunities. In *Rethinking violence against women*, ed. R.E. Dobash and R. P. Dobash, 1–22. Thousand Oaks, CA: Sage.

Dobash, R. P., R. E. Dobash, K. Cavanagh, and R. Lewis. 1998. Separate and intersecting realities: A comparison of men's and women's accounts of violence against women. *Violence Against Women* 4, 4: 382–414.

Dobash, R. E., R. P. Dobash, K. Cavanagh, and R. Lewis. 2000. *Changing violent men.* Thousand Oaks, CA: Sage.

Dobash, R. P., R. E. Dobash, M. Wilson, and M. Daly. 1992. The myth of sexual symmetry in marital violence. *Social Problems* 39, 1: 71–91.

Dragiewicz, M. 2008. Patriarchy reasserted: Fathers' rights and anti-VAWA activism. *Feminist Criminology* 3, 2: 121–44.

Dragiewicz, M., and Y. Lindgren. 2009. The gendered nature of domestic violence: Statistical data for lawyers considering equal protection analysis. *American University Journal of Gender, Social Policy and the Law* 17, 2: 229–68.

Dugan, L., D. S. Nagin, and R. Rosenfeld. 1999. Explaining the decline in intimate partner homicide: The effects of changing domesticity, women's status, and domestic violence resources. *Homicide Studies* 3, 3: 187–214.

Dunn, K. 1994. Truth abuse: The media's wife beating hype. *The New Republic,* August 1, 16–18.

Dutton, D. G. 1986. Wife assaulters' explanations for assault: The neutralization of self-punishment. *Canadian Journal of Behavioral Science* 18: 381–90.

Dutton, D. G. 1988. *The domestic assault of women: Psychological and criminal justice perspectives.* Newton, MA: Allyn and Bacon.

Dutton, D. G. 1994. Patriarchy and wife assault: The ecological fallacy. *Violence and Victims* 9: 167-82.

Dutton, D. G. 2006. *Rethinking domestic violence.* Vancouver: University of British Columbia Press.

Easteal, P. W. 1993. *Killing the beloved: Homicide between adult sexual intimates.* Canberra: Australian Institute of Technology.

Edleson, J. L., and M. P. Brygger. 1986. Gender differences in self-reporting of battering incidents: The impact of treatment upon reliability one year later. *Family Relations* 35: 377–82.

Edleson, J. L., and R. M. Tolman. 1992. *Intervention for men who batter: An ecological approach.* Newbury Park, CA: Sage.

Eisikovits, Z., and E. Buchbinder. 1997. Talking violent: A phenomenological study of metaphors battering men use. *Violence Against Women* 3, 5: 482–98.

Erickson, L. 1999. *Minnesota homicides 1985 to 1997.* St. Paul: Minnesota Planning.

Faludi, S. 1991. *Backlash: The undeclared war against American women.* New York: Anchor Books.

Fawcett, J., K. Starr, and A. Patel. 2008. *Now that we know: Findings and recommendations from the Washington State domestic violence fatality review.* Seattle: Washington State Coalition against Domestic Violence.

FCC v. Beach Communications, Inc., 508 U.S. 307 (1993).

Federal Bureau of Investigation. 2004. Supplementary homicide report. Federal Bureau of Investigation, http://www.fbi.gov/hq/cjisd/forms/homicidesup .pdf.

Fekete, J. 1994. *Moral panic: Biopolitics rising.* Montreal: Robert Davies.

Ferguson v. Skrupa, 372 U.S. 726 (1963).

Ferraro, K. 1996. The dance of dependency: A genealogy of domestic violence discourse. *Hypatia* 11, 4: 77–91.

Fiebert, M. 1997. References examining assaults by women on their spouses or male partners: An annotated bibliography. *Sexuality and Culture* 1: 273–86.

Fineman, M. A. 1994. Preface. In *The public nature of private violence: The discovery of domestic abuse,* ed. M. A. Fineman and R. Mykitiuk, xi-xviii. New York: Routledge.

Finkelhor, D., and K. Yllö. 1985. *License to rape: Sexual abuse of wives.* New York: Holt, Rinehart and Winston.

Finn, G. 1989. Taking gender into account in the 'theatre of terror': Violence, media and the maintenance of male dominance. *Canadian Journal of Women and the Law* 3, 2: 375–94.

Fishman, J. R., J. G. Wick, and B. A. Koenig. 1999. The use of "sex" and "gender" to define and characterize meaningful differences between men and women. *Agenda for Research on Women's Health for the 21st Century* 2: 15–20.

Fleury, R. E., C. M. Sullivan, and D. I. Bybee. 2000. When ending the relationship does not end the violence: Women's experiences of violence by former partners. *Violence Against Women* 6, 12: 1363–83.

Flood, M. 1999. Claims about husband battering, http://www.xyonline.net/content/claims-about-husband-battering.

Flood, M. 2010. "Fathers' rights" and the defense of paternal authority in Australia. *Violence Against Women* 16, 3: 328–47.

Flynn, C. P. 1990. Relationship violence by women: Issues and implications. *Family Relations* 39, 2: 194–98.

Foucault, M. 1972. *The archaeology of knowledge*. London: Tavistock.

Foucault, M. 1987. Questions of method: An interview with Michel Foucault. In *After philosophy: End or transformation?*, ed. K. Baynes, J. Bohman, and T. McCarthy, 100–117. Cambridge, MA: MIT Press.

Fox, B. J. 1993. On violent men and female victims: A comment on DeKeseredy and Kelly. *Canadian Journal of Sociology* 18, 3: 321–24.

Fox, J. A., and M. W. Zawitz. 2010. *Homicide trends in the U.S.: Intimate homicide*. Washington, DC: Bureau of Justice Statistics, Department of Justice, http://bjs.ojp.usdoj.gov/content/homicide/intimates.cfm.

Frederick, L. 2001. Brief of amici curiae, *Booth v. Hvass*, 302 F.3d 849 (8th Cir. 2002).

Free Republic. 2005. *Male battering—A serious problem*. Free Republic, http://www.freerepublic.com/focus/news/1374080/posts.

Frieze, I. H. 2000. Violence in close relationships—Development of a research area: Comment on Archer (2000). *Psychological Bulletin* 126, 5: 681–84.

Frye, M. 1983. *The politics of reality: Essays in feminist theory*. Berkeley, CA: Crossing Press.

Fukuroda, M. L. 2005. *Murder at home: An examination of legal and community responses to intimate femicide in California*. Los Angeles: California Women's Law Center.

Gabbard, G. O., and J. Larson. 1981. Masochism: Myth or human need? *American Journal of Psychiatry* 138, 4: 533.

Garcia, L., C. Soria, and E. L. Hurwitz. 2007. Homicides and intimate partner violence: A literature review. *Trauma, Violence and Abuse* 8, 4: 370–83.

Garrett, S. 2003. Battered by equality: Could Minnesota's domestic violence statutes survive a "fathers' rights" assault? *Law and Inequality: A Journal of Theory and Practice* 21, 2: 341–66.

Gartner, R. 1993. Studying woman abuse: A comment on DeKeseredy and Kelly. *Canadian Journal of Sociology* 18, 3: 313–20.

Gelles, R. J. 1997. *Intimate violence in families.* 3rd ed. Thousand Oaks, CA: Sage.

Gelles, R. J. 1999. Domestic violence: Not an even playing field. The Safety Zone, http://web.archive.org/web/20011219203436/http://www.serve.com/zone/everyone/gelles.html.

Minnesota Legal Services Coalition. 1998. Getting court orders for protection from abuse and harassment. 3rd ed. St. Paul: Minnesota Legal Services Coalition.

Gilbert, P. R. 2002. Discourses of female violence and societal gender stereotypes. *Violence Against Women* 8, 11: 1271–1300.

Gilligan, J. 1997. *Violence: Reflections on a national epidemic.* New York: Vintage Books.

Gilligan, J. 2001. *Preventing violence.* New York: Thames and Hudson.

Girard, A. L. 2009. Backlash or equality? The influence of men's and women's rights discourse on domestic violence legislation in Ontario. *Violence Against Women* 15, 1: 5–23.

Godenzi, A., M. D. Schwartz, and W. S. DeKeseredy. 2001. Toward a gendered social bond/male peer support theory of university woman abuse. *Critical Criminology* 10: 1–16.

Goetting, A. 1988. Patterns of homicide among women. *Journal of Interpersonal Violence* 3, 1: 3–20.

Goffman, E. 1974. *Frame analysis: An essay on the organization of experience.* New York: Harper and Row.

Gondolf, E. 1988. Who are these guys? Toward a behavioral typology of batterers. *Violence and Victims* 3, 3: 187–203.

Gordon, L. 1988. *Heroes of their own lives: The politics and history of family violence: Boston, 1880–1960.* New York: Viking.

Gwartney-Gibbs, P. A., J. Stockard, and S. Bohmer. 1983. Learning courtship aggression: The influence of parents, peers, and personal experiences. *Family Relations* 36, 3: 276–82.

Hamberger, L. K., and C. E. Guse. 2002. Men's and women's use of intimate partner violence in clinical samples. *Violence Against Women* 8, 11: 1301–31.

Hardesty, J. L. 2002. Separation assault in the context of postdivorce parenting: An integrative review of the literature. *Violence Against Women* 8, 5: 597–625.

Harper, D. W., and L. Voigt. 2007. Homicide followed by suicide: An integrated theoretical perspective. *Homicide Studies* 11, 4: 295–318.

Hearn, J. 1998. *The violences of men: How men talk about and how agencies respond to men's violence to women.* Thousand Oaks, CA: Sage.

Heise, L. L. 1998. Violence against women: An integrated, ecological framework. *Violence Against Women* 4, 3: 262–90.

Hilberman, E. 1980. Overview: The 'wife beater's wife' reconsidered. *American Journal of Psychiatry* 137: 1336–47.

Hoff Sommers, C. 1994. Figuring out feminism: How feminists abuse statistical information to serve their political agenda. *National Review,* June 27, 30–34.

hooks, b. 1984. *Feminist theory: From margin to center.* Boston: South End Press.

Howe, A. 1997. "The war against women": Media representations of men's violence against women in Australia. *Violence Against Women* 3, 1: 59–75.

In-Cites. 2006. *Violence Against Women:* An interview with Claire Renzetti. In-Cites, December, http://www.in-cites.com/journals/ ViolenceAgainstWomen.html.

Intersex Society of North America. 2009. What is intersex? Intersex Society of North America, http://www.isna.org/faq/what_is_intersex.

Johnson, A. G. 2005. *The gender knot: Unraveling our patriarchal legacy.* Rev. ed. Philadelphia: Temple University Press.

Johnson, H. 1995. Response to allegations about the violence against women survey. In *Wife assault and the Canadian criminal justice system,* ed. M. Valverde, L. MacLeod, and K. Johnson, 148–56. Toronto, ON: Centre of Criminology, University of Toronto.

Johnson, H. 1996. *Dangerous domains: Violence against women in Canada.* Toronto, ON: Nelson.

Johnson, J. L., L. Greaves, and R. Repta. 2009. Better science with sex and gender: Facilitating the use of a sex and gender-based analysis in health research. *International Journal for Equity in Health* 8, 14: 1–11.

Johnson, M. P. 1995. Patriarchal terrorism and common couple violence: Two forms of violence against women. *Journal of Marriage and Family* 57, 2: 283–94.

Johnson, M. P., and K. J. Ferraro. 2000. Research on domestic violence in the 1990s: Making distinctions. *Journal of Marriage and the Family* 62, 4: 948–63.

Jones, Ann. 1994. Crimes against women: Media part of problem for masking violence in the language of love. *USA Today,* March 10, A4.

Jouriles, E. N., and K. D. O'Leary. 1985. Interspousal reliability of reports of marital violence. *Journal of Consulting and Clinical Psychology* 53, 3: 419–21.

Jurik, N., and R. Winn. 1990. Gender and homicide: A comparison of men and women who kill. *Violence and Victims* 5, 4: 227–42.

Katz, J., and S. Jhally. 1999. *Tough guise: Violence, media and the crisis in masculinity.* DVD. Media Education Foundation.

Kaye, M., and J. Tolmie. 1998. Discoursing dads: The rhetorical devices of fathers' rights groups. *Melbourne University Law Review* 22: 162–94.

Kellermann, A. L., and J. A. Mercy. 1992. Men, women and murder: Gender specific differences in rates of fatal violence and victimization. *Journal of Trauma* 33, 1: 1–5.

Kelly, K. D. 1994. The politics of data. *Canadian Journal of Sociology* 19, 1: 81–85.

Kerber, L. K. 1998. *No constitutional right to be ladies: Women and the obligations of citizenship*. New York: Hill and Wang.

Kimmel, M. S. 2002. "Gender symmetry" in domestic violence: A substantive and methodological research review. *Violence Against Women* 8, 11: 1332–63.

Klein, D. 1997. An agenda for reading and writing about women, crime and justice. *Social Pathology* 3, 2: 81–91.

Korematsu v. United States, 323 U.S. 214 (1944).

Koss, M. P. 1993. Detecting the scope of rape: A review of prevalence research methods. *Journal of Interpersonal Violence* 8, 2: 198–222.

Koss, M. P., C. A. Gidycz, and N. Wisniewski. 1987. The scope of rape: incidence and prevalence of sexual aggression and victimization in a national sample of higher education students. *Journal of Consulting and Clinical Psychology* 55, 2: 162–70.

Kurz, D. 1989. Old problems and new directions in the study of violence against women. In *Issues in intimate violence*, ed. R. K. Bergen, 197–208. Thousand Oaks, CA: Sage.

Kurz, D. 1993. Physical assaults by husbands: A major social problem. In *Current controversies on family violence*, ed. R. J. Gelles and D. R. Loseke, 88–103. Newbury Park, CA: Sage.

Kurz, D. 1996. Separation, divorce, and woman abuse. *Violence Against Women* 2, 1: 63–81.

Lamb, S. 1991. Acts without agents: An analysis of linguistic avoidance in journal articles on men who batter women. *American Journal of Orthopsychiatry* 61, 2: 250–57.

Landenburger, K. 1989. A process of entrapment in and recovery from an abusive relationship. *Issues in Mental Health Nursing* 10, 3-4: 207–27.

Laney, G. P. 2005. Violence Against Women Act: History and federal funding. CRS Report for Congress. Washington, DC: Library of Congress.

Legal Action Committee. 2001a. Domestic violence: Challenging the Minnesota battered women's act. Legal Action Committee, http://web.archive.org/web/20050321174507/http://members.thebestisp.com/~sbooth/Domestic+Violence.htm.

Legal Action Committee. 2001b. Minnesota's battered women's act challenged. Legal Action Committee, http://web.archive.org/web/20050321131751/http://members.thebestisp.com/~sbooth/BWA+index.htm.

Leo, J. 1994. Is it a war against women? *U.S. News and World Report,* July 11, 22.

Leonard, E. D. 2002. Convicted survivors: The imprisonment of battered women who kill. Albany: State University of New York Press.

Lerman, L. G. 1992. The decontextualization of domestic violence. *Journal of Criminal Law and Criminology* 83, 1: 217–40.

Mann, R. M. 2008. Men's rights and feminist advocacy in Canadian domestic violence policy arenas: Contexts, dynamics, and outcomes of antifeminist backlash. *Feminist Criminology* 3, 1: 44–75.

Martin, D. 1981. *Battered wives.* Rev. ed. Volcano, CA: Volcano Press.

McCarry, M. J. 2009. Justifications and contradictions: Understanding young people's views of domestic abuse. *Men and Masculinities* 11, 3: 325–45.

McCarthy, S. 1994-95. The role of the media in domestic violence cases: A journalist's perspective. *Albany Law Review* 58: 1235–44.

McElroy, W. 1995. The unfair sex? Efforts to stop violence against women portray men unfairly. *National Review,* May 1, 74–76.

McKay, J., and P. Smith. 1995. Exonerating the hero: Frames and narratives in media coverage of the O. J. Simpson story. *Media Information Australia* 75: 57–66.

McNeely, R. L., and C. R. Mann. 1990. Domestic violence is a human issue. *Journal of Interpersonal Violence* 5, 1: 129–32.

McNeely, R. L., and G. Robinson-Simpson. 1987. The truth about domestic violence: A falsely framed issue. *Social Work* 32: 485–90.

McNeely, R. L., and G. Robinson-Simpson. 1988. The truth about domestic violence revisited: A reply to Saunders. *Social Work* 33: 184–88.

Men's rights blog. 2009. Roy, part 2, http://mensrightsboard.blogspot.com/ 2009_04_01_archive.html.

Menweb. 2010. Battered men—The hidden side of domestic violence, http:// www.batteredmen.com/bathelp.htm.

Menzies, R. 2007. Virtual backlash: Representations of men's "rights" and feminist "wrongs" in cyberspace. In *Reaction and resistance: Feminism, law, and social change*, ed. D. E. Chunn, S. B. Boyd, and H. Lessard, 65–97. Vancouver: University of British Columbia Press.

Messerschmidt, J. W. 1993. *Masculinities and crime: Critique and reconceptualization of theory.* Lanham, MD: Rowman and Littlefield.

Messerschmidt, J. W. 1997. *Crime as structured action: Gender, race, class, and crime in the making.* Thousand Oaks, CA: Sage Publications.

Messerschmidt, J. W. 1999. Making bodies matter: Adolescent masculinities, the body, and varieties of violence. *Theoretical Criminology* 3, 2: 197–220.

Messerschmidt, J. W. 2000. *Nine lives: Adolescent masculinities, the body, and violence.* Boulder, CO: Westview Press.

Messerschmidt, J. W. 2004. *Flesh and blood: Adolescent gender diversity and violence.* Lanham, MD.: Rowman and Littlefield.

Messner, M. A. 2000. *Politics of masculinities: Men in movements.* Lanham, MD: AltaMira Press.

Meyers, M. 1997. *News coverage of violence against women: Engendering blame.* Thousand Oaks, CA: Sage.

Miller, S. L. 1994. Expanding the boundaries: Toward a more inclusive and integrated study of intimate violence. *Violence and Victims* 9, 2: 183–94.

Millett, K. 1969. *Sexual politics.* New York: Avon.

Moore, T. M., and G. L. Stuart. 2005. A review of the literature on masculinity and partner violence. *Psychology of Men and Masculinity* 6, 1: 46–61.

Mullaney, J. L. 2007. Telling it like a man: masculinities and battering men's accounts of their violence. *Men and Masculinities* 10, 2: 222–47.

National Women's Law Center (2001). The Supreme Court and women's rights: Fundamental protections hang in the balance. National Women's Law Center, http://www.nwlc.org/pdf/SupremeCourtReport2003.pdf.

Nazroo, J. 1995. Uncovering gender differences in the use of marital violence: The effect of methodology. *Sociology* 29, 3: 475–94.

Nollet v. Justices of Trial Court of Com. of Mass., 248 F.3d 1127 (1st Cir. 2000).

O'Leary, K. D. 2000. Are women really more aggressive than men in intimate relationships? Comment on Archer. *Psychological Bulletin* 126, 5: 685–89.

Osthoff, S. 2002. But, Gertrude, I beg to differ, a hit is not a hit is not a hit: When battered women are arrested for assaulting their partners. *Violence Against Women* 8, 12: 1521–44.

Osthoff, S., S. D. Dasgupta, and A. Bible. 2002. Guest editors' introduction. *Violence Against Women* 8, 11: 1267–70.

Pagelow, M. 1981. *Woman battering: Victims and their experiences.* Newbury Park, CA: Sage.

Parsons, T. 1947. Certain primary sources and patterns of aggression in the social structure of the Western world. *Psychiatry* 10, 2: 167–81.

Pearson, P. 1997. *When she was bad: Violent women and the myth of innocence.* New York: Viking Adult.

Pence, E., and M. Paymar. 1993. *Education groups for men who batter: The Duluth model.* New York: Springer Publishing.

Pharr, S. 1987. *Homophobia: A weapon of sexism.* Berkeley, CA: Chardon Press.

Phillips, D., and D. Henderson. 1999. 'Patient was hit in the face by a fist . . .': A discourse analysis of male violence against women. *American Journal of Orthopsychiatry* 69, 1: 116–21.

Phillips, S. P. 2005. Defining and measuring gender: A social determinant of health whose time has come. *International Journal for Equity in Health* 4, 11: 1–4.

Pizzey, E. 2006. Domestic violence is not a gender issue. ifeminists.com, http://www.ifeminists.net/introduction/editorials/2006/0719pizzey.html.

Plaintiffs' answer to interrogatories. 2001. *Booth v. Hvass*, 302 F.3d 849 (8th Cir. 2002).

Plaintiffs' omnibus answer to motions of the defendants and the intervenors and to the submission of the amici curiae. 2001. *Booth v. Hvass*, 302 F.3d 849 (8th Cir. 2002).

Pleck, E. 1987. *Domestic tyranny: The making of American social policy against family violence from colonial times to the present.* New York: Oxford University Press.

Pleck, E., J. Pleck, M. Grossman, and P. Bart. 1977–78. The battered data syndrome: A comment on Steinmetz's article. *Victimology* 2, 3/4: 680–83.

Pozner, J. 1999. Not all domestic violence studies are created equal. *Fair,* November/December, http://www.fair.org/index.php?page=1479.

Presser, L. 2003. Remorse and neutralization among violent male offenders. *Justice Quarterly* 20, 4: 801–25.

Pryzgoda, J., and J. C. Chrisler. 2000. Definitions of gender and sex: The subtleties of meaning. *Sex Roles* 43, 7/8: 553-69.

Ptacek, J. 1990. Why do men batter their wives? In *Feminist perspectives on wife abuse,* ed. K.Yllö and M. Bograd, 133–57. Newbury Park, CA: Sage.

Puzone, C. A., L. E. Saltzman, M.-J. Kresnow, M. P. Thompson, and J. A. Mercy. 2000. National trends in intimate partner homicide: United States, 1976–1995. *Violence Against Women* 6, 4: 409–26.

Rand, M. R. 2008. *Criminal victimization, 2007.* Washington, DC: US Department of Justice, Office of Justice Programs.

Reitzel-Jaffe, D., and D. A. Wolfe. 2001. Predictors of relationship abuse among young men. *Journal of Interpersonal Violence* 16, 2: 99–115.

Rennison, C. M. 2002. *Rape and sexual assault: Reporting to police and medical attention, 1992–2000.* Washington, DC: Bureau of Justice Statistics.

Renzetti, C. M. 1994. On dancing with a bear: Reflections on some of the current debates among domestic violence theorists. *Violence and Victims* 9, 2: 195–200.

Rich, A. 1980. Compulsory heterosexuality and lesbian existence. *Signs* 5, 4: 631–60.

R-KIDS. 1999. R-KIDS director meeting notes. R-KIDS, http://web.archive.org/web/20010303103526/http://r-kids.org/n11099.html.

R-KIDS. 2001. R-KIDS and grandparents newsletter. R-KIDS, http://www.r-kids.org/n11001.htm.

Robinson, V. 1994. Denial and patriarchy: The relationship between patriarchy and woman abuse. In *Conflict and gender,* ed. A.Taylor and J. B. Miller, 25–44. Cresskill, NJ: Hampton Press.

Rosen, L. 2006. Origin and goals of the "gender symmetry" workshop. *Violence Against Women* 12, 11: 997–1002.

Rosen, L. N., M. Dragiewicz, and J. C. Gibbs. 2009. Fathers' rights groups: Demographic correlates and impact on custody policy. *Violence Against Women* 15, 5: 513–31.

Rosenfeld, R. 1997. Changing relationships between men and women: A note on the decline in intimate partner homicide. *Homicide Studies* 1, 1: 72–83.

Russell, D. E. H. 1982. *Rape in marriage.* New York: Macmillan.

Saunders, D. G. 1986. When battered women use violence: Husband abuse or self defense? *Violence and Victims* 1, 1: 47–60.

Saunders, D. G. 1988. Other "truths" about domestic violence: A reply to McNeely and Robinson-Simpson. *Social Work* 33, 2: 179–83.

Saunders, D. G. 1990. Wife abuse, husband abuse, or mutual combat? A feminist perspective on the empirical findings. In *Feminist perspectives on wife abuse*, ed. K. Yllö and M. Bograd, 90–113. Newbury Park, CA: Sage.

Saunders, D. G. 2001. Affidavit for *Booth v. Hvass*, 302 F.3d 849 (8th Cir. 2002).

Saunders, D. G. 2002. Are physical assaults by wives and girlfriends a major social problem? A review of the literature. *Violence Against Women* 8, 12: 1424–48.

Schechter, S. 1982. *Women and male violence: The visions and struggles of the battered women's movement.* Boston: South End Press.

Schneider, E. 2000. *Battered women and feminist lawmaking.* New Haven, CT: Yale University Press.

Schwartz, M. D. 1987. Gender and injury in spousal assault. *Sociological Focus* 20, 1: 61–75.

Schwartz, M. D. 2000. Methodological issues in the use of survey data for measuring and characterizing violence against women. *Violence Against Women* 6, 8: 815–38.

Schwartz, M. D., and W. S. DeKeseredy. 1993. The return of the 'battered husband syndrome' through the typification of women as violent. *Crime, Law and Social Change* 20, 3: 249–65.

Schwartz, M. D. and W. S. DeKeseredy. 1997. *Sexual assault on the college campus: The role of male peer support.* Thousand Oaks, CA: Sage.

Scully, D., and J. A. Marolla. 1985. Riding the bull at Gilley's: Convicted rapists describe the rewards of rape. *Social Problems* 32, 3: 251–63.

Silverman, J. G., and G. M. Williamson. 1997. Social ecology and entitlements involved in battering by heterosexual college males: Contributions of family and peers. *Violence and Victims* 12, 2: 147–64.

Smith, M. D. 1987. The incidence and prevalence of woman abuse in Toronto. *Violence and Victims* 2, 3: 173–87.

Smith, M. D. 1990. Patriarchal ideology and wife beating: A test of a feminist hypothesis. *Violence and Victims* 5, 4: 257–73.

Smith, M. D. 1991. Male peer support of wife abuse: An exploratory study. *Journal of Interpersonal Violence* 6, 4: 512–19.

Snell, J. E., R. J. Rosenwald, and A. Robey. 1964. The wifebeater's wife: A study of family interaction. *Archives of General Psychiatry* 11, 2: 107–12.

Stamp, G. H., and T. C. Sabourin. 1995. Accounting for violence: An analysis of male spousal abuse narratives. *Journal of Applied Communication Research* 23, 4: 284–307.

Stark, E. 2007. *Coercive control: How men entrap women in personal life.* New York: Oxford University Press.

Steeves, H. L. 1997. *Gender violence and the press: The St. Kizito story*. Athens: Ohio University Center for International Studies.

Steinmetz, S. K. 1977–78. The battered husband syndrome. *Victimology: An International Journal* 2, 3/4: 499–509.

Stone, S. D. 1993. Getting the message out: Feminists, the press, and violence against women. *Canadian Review of Sociology and Anthropology* 30, 3: 377–400.

Straus, M. A. 1979. Measuring family conflict and violence: The Conflict Tactics Scales. *Journal of Marriage and the Family* 41: 75–88.

Straus, M. A. 1990a. Injury and frequency of assault and the 'representative sample fallacy' in measuring wife beating and child abuse. In *Physical violence in American families: Risk factors and adaptations to violence in 8,154 families*, ed. M. A. Straus and R. J. Gelles, 75–91. New Brunswick, NJ: Transaction Publishers.

Straus, M. A. 1990b. The Conflict Tactics Scales and its critics: An evaluation and new data on validity and reliability. In *Physical violence in American families: Risk factors and adaptations to violence in 8,154 families*, ed. M. A. Straus and R. J. Gelles, 49–73. New Brunswick, NJ: Transaction Publishers.

Straus, M. A. 1993. Physical assaults by wives: A major social problem. In *Current controversies on family violence*, ed. R. J. Gelles and D. R. Loseke, 67–87. Newbury Park, CA: Sage.

Straus, M. A., S. L. Hamby, S. Boney-McCoy, and D. B. Sugarman. 1996. The revised Conflict Tactics Scales (CTS-2): Development and preliminary psychometric data. *Journal of Family Issues* 17, 3: 283-316.

Straus, M. A., R. J. Gelles, and S. K. Steinmetz. 1981. *Behind closed doors: Violence in the American family*. Garden City, NY: Anchor Books.

Strom, K. J. 2000. Using hospital emergency room data to assess intimate violence-related injuries. *Justice Research and Policy* 2, 1: 2–20.

Szinovacz, M. 1983. Using couple data as a methodological tool: The case of marital violence. *Journal of Marriage and the Family* 45: 633–44.

Thompson, J. B. 1995. No cause for joy: A womanist response to the O.J. trial and its aftermath. *The Black Scholar* 25, 4: 56–59.

Tigner v. Texas, 310 U.S. 141 (1940).

Tjaden, P., and N. Thoennes. 1998. *Stalking in America: Findings from the National Violence Against Women Survey*. Washington, DC: National Institute of Justice, Centers for Disease Control and Prevention.

Tjaden, P., and N. Thoennes. 2000. *Extent, nature, and consequences of intimate partner violence: Findings from the National Violence Against Women Survey*. Washington, DC: National Institute of Justice, Centers for Disease Control and Prevention.

Tjaden, P., and N. Thoennes. 2006. *Extent, nature, and consequences of rape victimization: Findings from the National Violence Against Women Survey*. Washington, DC: National Institute of Justice.

Toby, J. 1966. Violence and the masculine ideal: Some qualitative data. *Annals of the American Academy of Political and Social Science* 364, 1: 19–27.

Totten, M. 2003. Girlfriend abuse as a form of masculinity construction. *Men and Masculinities* 6, 1: 70–92.

U.S. Constitution Amendment XIV, §1.

Valente, R. L., B. J. Hart, S. Zeya, and M. Malefyt. 2001. The Violence Against Women Act of 1994: The federal commitment to ending domestic violence, sexual assault, stalking, and gender-based crimes of violence. In *Sourcebook on violence against women*, ed. C. M. Renzetti, J. L. Edleson, and R. K. Bergen, 279–302. Thousand Oaks, CA: Sage.

Victims of Trafficking and Violence Protection Act of 2000 (VAWA 2000), Div. B, Public Law 106–386, 106th Cong., 2d sess. (January 24, 2000), Section 1001 et. Seq.

Violence Against Women and Department of Justice Reauthorization Act of 2005 (VAWA 2005), Public Law 109–162, 109th Cong., 1st sess. (January 4, 2005), Section 1 et. Seq.

Violence Policy Center. 2008. *American roulette: Murder suicide in the United States.* 3rd ed. Washington, D.C. Violence Policy Center, http://www.vpc.org/studies/amrou12008.pdf.

Violent Crime Control and Law Enforcement Act of 1994 (VAWA), Public Law 103–322, 103rd Cong., 2d sess. (January 25, 1994), Title IV, Section 40001 et. Seq.

Walby, S. 1990. *Theorizing patriarchy.* Oxford, UK: Basil Blackwell.

Walby, S. 1993. Backlash in historical context. In *Making connections: Women's studies, women's movements, women's lives*, ed. M. Kennedy, C. Lubelska, and V. Walsh, 79–89. Washington, DC: Taylor and Francis.

Websdale, N. 1998. *Rural woman battering and the criminal justice system: An ethnography.* Thousand Oaks, CA: Sage.

Websdale, N. 1999. *Understanding domestic homicide.* Thousand Oaks, CA: Sage.

Websdale, N., and A. Alvarez. 1997. Forensic journalism as patriarchal ideology: The media construction of domestic homicide-suicide. In *Popular culture, crime and justice*, ed. F. Y. Bailey and D.C. Hale, 123–41. Belmont, CA: Wadsworth.

Websdale, N., and M. Chesney-Lind. 1998. Doing violence to women: Research synthesis on the victimization of women. In *Masculinities and violence*, ed. L. Bowker, 55–81. Thousand Oaks, CA: Sage.

Weedon, C. 1987. *Feminist practice and poststructuralist theory.* Malden, MA: Blackwell.

Weiss, K. G. 2009. "Boys will be boys" and other gendered accounts: An exploration of victims' excuses and justifications for unwanted sexual contact and coercion. *Violence Against Women* 15, 7: 810–34.

White, J. W., P. H. Smith, M. P. Koss, and A. J. Figueredo. 2000. Intimate partner aggression: What have we learned? Comment on Archer (2000). *Psychological Bulletin* 126, 5: 697–702.

Williams, G. I., and R. H. Williams. 1995. "All we want is equality": Rhetorical framing in the fathers' rights movement. In *Images of issues: Typifying contemporary social problems*, ed. J. Best, 191–212. New York: Aldine de Gruyter.

Williamson, G. M., and J. G. Silverman. 2001. Violence against female partners: Direct and interactive effects of family history, communal orientation, and peer-related variables. *Journal of Social and Personal Relationships* 18, 4: 535–49.

Wilson, M., and M. Daly. 1992. Who kills whom in spouse killings? On the exceptional ratio of spousal homicides in the United States. *Criminology* 30: 189–215.

Wilson, M., and M. Daly. 1993. Spousal homicide risk and estrangement. *Violence and Victims* 8, 1: 3–16.

Wilson, M., M. Daly, and A. Daniele. 1995. Familicide: The killing of spouse and children. *Aggressive Behavior* 21: 275–91.

Wood, J. T. 2001. The normalization of violence in heterosexual romantic relationships: Women's narratives of love and violence. *Journal of Social and Personal Relationships* 18, 2: 239–61.

Woods v. Horton, 167 Cal. App. 4th 658, 84 Cal. Rptr. 3d 332 (2008).

World Health Organization. 2002. *World report on violence and health: Summary.* Geneva: World Health Organization.

Yllö, K. 1990. Political and methodological debates in wife abuse research. In *Feminist perspectives on wife abuse*, ed. K.Yllö and M. Bograd, 28–50. Newbury Park, CA: Sage.

Yllö, K., and M. Bograd, eds. *Feminist perspectives on wife abuse.* Newbury Park, CA: Sage.

Young, C. 1994. Abused statistics; like hydra heads or spreading kudzu, the false statistics keep proliferating. *National Review,* August 1, 43–46.

Zick, T. 2000/2001. Angry white males: The equal protection clause and "classes of one." *Kentucky Law Journal* 89: 69–135.

Index

Kahn, Phyllis, 40–42
Katz, Jackson, 105
Kaye, Miranda, 21–22
Kimmel, M. S., 89
Koenig, Barbara, 104
Korematsu v. United States, 33
Kozol, Wendy, 54–55

Lamb, Sharon, 58
Landsman, Maury, 44
Larson, Jan, 63
law enforcement: crime and deviance
    discourses, 13, 55–58; nonintervention
    in domestic disputes, 47–48, 110
liberal feminism, 15

marital rape, 30
Marolla, Joseph, 62
masculinity: in batterer narratives,
    61–62, 68, 71, 76–77, 79; need for
    future research, 121; violence as
    affirmation of, 109, 112–17
masochism, accusation of female, 40, 63
McCarthy, Sheryl, 54
media: antifeminist articles in main-
    stream outlets, 51–52; bias in lan-
    guage reporting on woman abuse, 51;
    individualization of woman abuse,
    54–55; journalistic pieces on sex
    symmetry, 86; sensationalized
    intimate partner violence stories,
    49–50; victim blaming in reporting,
    54, 59–60
men: claims about denial of service to,
    45–46; discrimination claims of, 27,
    37–38, 40–42; and ecological model
    of intimate partner violence, 21;
    invisibility as perpetrators, 58, 64;
    social normalization of violence for,
    47, 116–17; as threatened by feminism,
    123; as victims of intimate partner
    violence, 31, 53–54, 85–86, 93–96,

99–101; vs. women as perpetrators,
    47, 84–85, 96, 121–22
Men's Defense Association, 1, 26
"men's rights" groups, 13–18
Menzies, Robert, 14
Meyers, Marian, 59
Millett, K., 107
minimization in batterer narratives,
    68–72
Moore, Ted, 112
multiple factor interaction (meso-
    system) in gender-based violence,
    20, 111–17, 119–21
mutual combat perspective on intimate
    partner violence, 60, 74–76, 80

Nagin, Daniel, 96
National Coalition of Free Men, Twin
    Cities Chapter, 1, 26
National Crime Victimization Survey
    (NCVS), 99
National Family Violence Survey
    (NFVS), 91–92
National Fatherhood Initiative, 16
National Violence Against Women
    Survey (NVAWS), 100
NCVS (National Crime Victimization
    Survey), 99
*News Coverage of Violence Against
    Women* (Meyers), 59
NFVS (National Family Violence
    Survey), 91–92
nominalization of violence, 71
nonintervention by police in domestic
    violence incidents, 47–48, 110

Olson, Karen, 44
orders for protection (OFP), 22–23, 35, 39

passion, domestic crimes of, social
    acceptability of, 51
pathologizing of woman abuse, 56

Schechter, Susan, 82, 85

Schwartz, Martin, 24, 92, 101, 114–15, 120

Scully, Diana, 62

self-defense, and intimate partner violence, 74–75, 96

separation assault, 38, 98–99

sex, vs. gender, 2, 5, 103–8, 118

sex differences, in intimate partner violence: evidence for, 93–101; implications of, 101–2; introduction, 81–87; multiple factors influencing, 117; sex symmetry argument by *Booth* plaintiffs, 29–31, 87–93; and societal norms, 103

sexism and patriarchy, 108, 109

sex symmetry claims: antifeminist groups' use of, 18, 33–35, 42–43, 64, 86; of *Booth* plaintiffs, 29–31, 87–93; higher visibility of, 84–85; refutation of, 44–48, 93–102, 118–20; and research, 11. *See also* gender-neutrality

sexual assault, sex differences in, 100

sexual preference, 107–8, 121–22

SHR (Supplementary Homicide Reporting) program, FBI, 94

Silverman, Jay, 114–16

Smith, Michael, 114

social ecology of woman abuse: and batterer narratives, 72, 74–76, 79; and contextualized vs. individualized approaches to violence, 48, 54–56; importance of multifactor models, 20, 82–83, 111–17, 119–21; and masculinity, 109, 112–17, 121; overview, 18–25; patriarchy's integral role in, 109–17. *See also* patriarchy

socialization level for man, and isolation of woman, 113–14

social norms: and excuse method in batterer narratives, 72–73; and

gender vs. biological sex, 104–7; heteronormativity, 107–8; and justification of violence, 74; and legal conflict, 4, 33; for masculinity, 61–62, 68, 71, 76–77, 79; promoting men's violence, 47, 116–17; violation of femininity norms as violence justification, 38, 76–77, 79, 110, 113, 117. *See also* social ecology of woman abuse

socioeconomic class, and woman abuse, 57–58, 114, 122

stalking, sex differences in, 99–100

Stamp, Glen, 65

status incompatibility in relationship, and violence, 111

Steinmetz, Suzanne, 85–86

Straus, Murray, 42, 81, 84, 87–92

strict level of scrutiny in equal protection law, 33

Strom, Kevin, 101

Stuart, Gregory, 112

sublethal injury, sex differences in, 98–101

Sullivan, Cris, 99

Supplementary Homicide Reporting (SHR) program, FBI, 94

survivors of domestic violence, resources information for, 39. *See also* battered women's movement; battered women's shelters

teens involved in abusive relationships, signs of, 39

Tennenhouse, Leonard, 5

terminology issues, 8–10, 108–9

Thoennes, N., 99

Tjaden, P., 99

Toby, Jackson, 113

Tolman, R. M., 20

Tolmie, Julia, 21–22

truth effects of discourse, 9